W9-CBD-340

THE RACE
TO SAVE THE WORLD

SID ROTH

Charisma
HOUSE
A STRANG COMPANY

THE RACE TO SAVE THE WORLD by Sid Roth
Published by Charisma House
A Strang Company
600 Rinehart Road
Lake Mary, Florida 32746
www.charismahouse.com

Cover design by Ededron Hernandez

Library of Congress Cataloging-in-Publication Data

Roth, Sid.
    The race to save the world / Sid Roth.
        p. cm.
    Includes bibliographical references.
    ISBN 1-59185-411-3 (pbk.)
    1. Bible--Prophecies. I. Title.
    BS647.3.R68 2004
    220.1'5--dc22

                                        2004008667

04 05 06 07 08 — 98765432
Printed in the United States of America

To my daughter, Leigh, and son-in-law, Greg Williamson.
Leigh is Jewish, and Greg is a Gentile.
Both know and love the Messiah of Israel.
Their first daughter is named Olivia
because she is the fruit of the
Jew and Gentile grafted into the Olive Tree.

Acknowledgments

I wish to thank Robert DuVall who has spent many hours editing the manuscript before and even during the editing process with Charisma House. He has been a trusted friend and a real "Timothy" to me over the years.

I am grateful to Charisma House editor Lillian McAnally. She took her assignment as from the Lord, and her labor of love moved the book to a new level of excellence.

Contents

Foreword

I met Sid Roth at a service in Jacksonville, Florida, where my wife, Kathy, and I were ministering. Sid was so hungry for a touch from God that he shook under the power of the Holy Spirit. As I've watched Sid over the years, I've seen his passion for the deeper things of the Lord increase the mantle to bring a fresh move of God into the Jewish community. Many of Sid's insights in this book bridge the great chasm between the church and the Jewish people. As the bridge is built bringing the Jewish and non-Jewish church together, we are prepared to take the next step in fulfilling God's purposes in this last hour.

Although the Jewish people are important to what God is doing in the earth, they have suffered greatly from anti-Semitism promulgated by some of the early church leaders. This book reveals the roots of anti-Semitism in the church and prophetically proclaims an outline for the next great move of God.

I agree wholeheartedly with Sid that the church is incomplete without Jewish believers coming together with non-Jewish believers as they did in the Book of Acts. Most Christians don't realize that the first apostles and leaders were Jews who evangelized the non-Jewish world. Now is the time for Gentiles to return the favor by letting the glory of God flow through us back to the Jewish people.

This book is part of something I have longed for and dreamed of for many years—to see Jewish apostles and prophets again walking the earth. As these Jewish leaders are raised up and released, we will see the End-Time church become "One New Man," manifesting the glory of God. Ephesians 4:4–6 (NLT) states:

> We are all one body, we have the same Spirit, and we have all been called to the same glorious future. There is only one Lord, one faith, one baptism, and there is only one God and Father, who is over us all and in us all and living through us all.

Messiah Jesus has broken down the middle wall of division between Jew and Gentile. (See Ephesians 2:14.) When the two come together creating One New Man, the glory will increase with healings, miracles, and the greatest harvest of souls in history.

—STEVE GRAY
WORLD REVIVAL CHURCH, KANSAS CITY, MISSOURI
(FORMER PASTOR OF THE SMITHTON OUTPOURING)

Introduction

The establishment of God's kingdom on earth is like a relay race. One man runs a lap and passes the baton to the next team member. The strongest runner—the anchor—runs the last lap.

Adam started the race but faltered. Abraham and his children (the Jewish people) then picked up the baton and ran the laps faithfully. But two thousand years ago, we Jewish people got very, very tired.

So we passed the baton to the Gentile Christians. After centuries of running with the gospel, they too are beginning to wear down. It's the last lap, and it doesn't look like our team is going to win.

Should the Gentile Christians pass the baton to the Messianic Jews (Jewish believers in Jesus)? No, they are stronger than ever, but not strong enough.

What then should the church do? A champion is needed if we are to win the race, and that champion is the "One New Man."

In this book, it is my goal to establish the fact that God never intended to start a new religion. It's not Judaism and Christianity, two streams of God, but the convergence of Jew and Gentile into one stream that I call the "One New Man."

God wants to "gather together in *one* all things in [Messiah]" (Eph. 1:10, emphasis added). He tells us how He will do this:

> For He Himself is our peace, who has made *both* [Jew and Gentile] *one*, and has broken down the middle wall of separation...to create in Himself *one new man*...in whom you also are being built together for a *dwelling place* of God in the Spirit.
> —EPHESIANS 2:14–15, 22, EMPHASIS ADDED

This book is divided into three sections.

The first part deals with God's champion, the Jews. This history includes the hidden intrigue of the rabbis, which still impacts Judaism today.

The second part deals with God's champion, the Christians. This history includes the hidden intrigue of the church fathers that still impacts the church today.

And the last part reveals God's winning strategy—His convergence of the Jew and Gentile into One New Man.

Jesus summarized this strategy in John 17:21 when He expressed His desire that "they [Jew and Gentile] all may be one...*that the world may believe...*"

(emphasis added). It will cause the same glory that is on Jesus to be on the One New Man. Jesus said:

> And the glory which You gave Me I have given them, that they may be one just as We are one.
> —JOHN 17:22

God is up to something new. It's bigger than Messianic Judaism. It's bigger than Gentile Christianity. Both have been used mightily by God, but this new move will not look like a traditional synagogue, a traditional church, or even a Messianic Jewish synagogue, although it will have aspects of each. It will not be the *one man show*, but the *One New Man*. It is Jewish *and* Gentile believers, holding the baton together. The two have been made one in Jesus—the second Adam. He is our Anchor, and in Him we win!

PART 1
ON YOUR MARK, SET...

"At the same time," says the LORD, "I will be the God of all the families of Israel, and they shall be My people."
—JEREMIAH 31:1

CHAPTER 1

"We Are Not Lost"

t is a miracle that Jewish people still exist today. After thousands of years of persecution, there should be none left. But God said as long as there is a sun and moon and stars, there will be a physical Jew on the face of the earth (Jer. 31:35–36).

We know that during IIis millennial reign, Jesus and His disciples will rule over the twelve tribes of Israel (Matt. 19:28). The ancient rabbis believed three things had to take place before the Messiah would appear. First, Israel had to be restored as a Jewish nation, which occurred in 1948. Second, the temple had to be rebuilt in Jerusalem. This could happen very quickly. And third, the ten lost tribes had to be restored to Israel (Jer. 31:7–11). This seemed impossible—until now.

Filmmaker Simcha Jacobovici, a traditional Jew, read about the locations where the lost tribes were scattered in Isaiah 11:11. He set up a scientific expedition to find and document the existence of these tribes. Not only did he find them exactly where God scattered them, but he discovered that they had not assimilated into their surrounding environment.

For example, he found descendants from the tribe of Manasseh living in northeast India. They observe the Sabbath, the festivals, and biblical Jewish laws. In 2000, the Israeli Ministry of the Interior granted citizenship to the first one hundred members of the tribe.

All ten "lost" tribes have been located. They say, "We are not lost!" Many of the tribes practice an aberrant form of Judaism, but all have relics and customs proving their heritage. I agree with them and the Word of God—they are not lost.

EVERLASTING COVENANT OF LOVE

God loves Israel. He made an everlasting covenant of love that nobody or nothing can break. In Romans 11:28–29, Paul states:

> Concerning the gospel [the Jewish people] are enemies for your sake [so Gentiles can be saved], but concerning the election they are beloved for the sake of the fathers. For the gifts and the calling of God are *irrevocable*.
>
> —EMPHASIS ADDED

God's covenant love for the Jewish people is evident in Hosea 11:1–4, 8:

> When Israel was a child,
> I loved him....
> They sacrificed to the Baals,
> And burned incense to carved images.
>
> I [God] taught Ephraim [Israel] to walk,
> Taking them by their arms....
> I drew them with gentle cords,
> With bands of love....
> I stooped and fed them....
> How can I give you up, Ephraim?...
> My heart churns within Me.

God is crying out to Israel:

> Return, O backsliding children...for I am married
> to you...and I will bring you to Zion [Israel].
> —JEREMIAH 3:14

If God refuses to violate His covenant love for His ancient Jewish people even in the face of their disobedience, imagine the love He has for His New Covenant people. Dear Christian, stop and contemplate how much God loves you. God says to the older brother (symbolic of the Gentile believer) in the parable of the prodigal son: "All that I have is yours" (Luke 15:31).

NO JEWS ALLOWED

Throughout history, people like Haman in the Book of Esther, Queen Isabella of Spain, and Hitler have cursed the Jew. Entire nations have come against the Jewish people. Even here in America—"the land of the free"—I remember as a young child a sign at the beach that read, "No Dogs or Blacks or Jews Allowed!" (Except it used a different word for "Blacks.")

What is the result of these curses against Jews? Jewish people as a whole are spiritually blind to the gospel message. The devil has backed the Jew into a corner. We have bitterness, pain, and hatred in our hearts. Our response is understandable. We blamed God for the Holocaust. We blamed Christians for our persecution. We are painfully aware of the tragic history of anti-Semitism among many church "fathers." Even for Jews who love God, these wounds are buried deep in our psyche.

How then can Christian believers reach the Jewish people with the gospel? One of the best methods is with a miracle of physical healing. But there is an even greater way. Malachi 4:5–6 says Elijah will prepare the way for the Messiah. The Spirit that was on Elijah will come on the church and allow it to walk in the pure love of God. Many spiritual "fathers" will be raised up. Their job will be to reveal the love of the heavenly Father *to the Jew first* and then the entire world. (See chapter 8.) Only the compassion of Father God will melt the deep bitterness in Jewish hearts.

STANDING WITH THE JEWISH PEOPLE

The Jews are the most love-starved people on the face of the earth: abused, misunderstood, persecuted, discriminated against, and murdered. We have a covenant with God, but most Jews do not know Him. As a result, many of my people are on the forefront of unbiblical positions such as pro-abortion, pro-homosexual rights, pro-New Age, and against school prayer. For the sake of fairness, many Jewish people have made scientific and medical discoveries that have brought great benefit to mankind.

The devil's strategy is to use the anti-God stances of some Jews to cause nominal Christians to join non-believers in hating *all* Jews. The world and *nominal* Christians will also hate genuine Christian believers. First they will hate them for standing with the Jew. Then they will hate them for standing with the Jewish Messiah. First the natural, then the spiritual. Christians need to heed the warning Mordecai gave Esther:

> Do not think in your heart that you will escape in the king's palace any more than all the other Jews. For if you remain silent at this time, relief and deliverance will arise for the Jews from another place, but you and your father's house will perish.
> —ESTHER 4:13–14

Standing with the Jew is not a popular decision, but if God is for you, who can be against you? God has faith in you. He is passionately and patiently

5

waiting for this last generation to demonstrate Isaiah 49:22–23:

> Thus says the Lord GOD:
>
> "Behold, I will lift My hand in an oath to the
>   nations [Gentiles],
> And set up My standard for the peoples;
> They shall bring your sons [Jewish people] in
>   their arms,
> And your daughters shall be carried on their
>   shoulders;
> *Kings* shall be your foster fathers,
> And their *queens* your nursing mothers;
> They shall bow down to you with their faces to
>   the earth,
> And lick up the dust of your feet.
> Then you will know that I am the LORD."
>
> —EMPHASIS ADDED

Jewish people will know Jesus is the Messiah when all Christian believers (kings and queens in God's kingdom) start acting like disciples (by embracing humility) and stop conforming to the world. The world will hate you, but the multitudes that will be in heaven because you obeyed God's commands will welcome you home.

CHAPTER 2

The Rabbinic Conspiracy

friend of mine, the pastor of a large
Charismatic church, had a supernatural
experience while he was visiting the Great
Synagogue in Jerusalem. As he was praying, Jesus
came to him and said, "I would be more at home in
this building than in your church."

Although there are many Gentile believers who are
longing for a deeper walk with God, many of them do
not recognize that a missing link is their biblical Jewish heritage. Is the solution to add Rabbinic Judaism to
our present dogma?

No. Simply put, Rabbinic Judaism has drifted far
from the Judaism of the Bible. Tradition in the church
may have isolated Christians from their Jewish roots
and from experiencing full intimacy and the power of

God (see chapter ten), but the tradition of the rabbis has separated Jewish people from their Messiah.

While the devil was deceiving the church leaders with anti-Semitic thoughts, he was corrupting the authority of the Scriptures in Judaism. Both groups were digging in and believing the big lie—you cannot be Jewish and believe in Jesus. The formula was simple. Give the rabbis authority *above* the Scriptures. Remove Jesus from Judaism, and separate the Christian from the Jew. This will stop the unlimited outpouring of God's glory, and the full revival will be aborted.

JUDAISM REPACKAGED

Let us examine how Rabbinic Judaism has tried to exclude Jesus. In the Great Revolt by Jewish zealots against Roman rule (A.D. 66–70), a million Jews were killed and the temple in Jerusalem was destroyed. Afterward, Yohanan ben Zakkai set about to reconstruct Judaism in Yavne on the coast of Israel. Why was this necessary? Because there was no temple, and they had rejected God's Messiah—the sacrifice that was made once for all. The Torah (first five books of the Old Covenant) clearly says that without the shedding of blood, there is no remission of sin (Lev. 17:11). Rather than accept the truth that animal sacrifices were a shadow of the ultimate Passover Lamb—the Messiah—who would take away all sin, ben Zakkai and his followers invented a new bloodless religion—Rabbinic Judaism.

The following quote illustrates the dramatic shift that took place within Judaism:

As Rabban Yohanan ben Zakkai was coming forth from Jerusalem, Rabbi Joshua followed after him and beheld the Temple in ruins. "Woe unto us!" Rabbi Joshua cried, "that this, the place where the iniquities of Israel were atoned for, is laid waste!" "My son," Rabban Yohanan said to him, "be not grieved; we have another atonement as effective as this. And what is it? It is acts of loving-kindness, as it is said, 'For I desire mercy and not sacrifice' [Hosea 6:6]" (Avot de Rabbi Nathan 4:18).[1]

At the end of his life, ben Zakkai finally realized his creation gave him no assurance of life after death. On his death bed, he said, "I have before me two roads, one to Paradise and one to Gehenna [hell], and I know not whether [God] will sentence me to Gehenna or admit me to Paradise" (Tractate Berachot 28b). A famous Rabbi once said, "If the blind leads the blind, both will fall into a ditch" (Matt. 15:14).

Rabbi Akiba ben Joseph studied the teachings of Yohanan ben Zakkai in Yavne and continued to build on his foundation. He created the structure of the Talmud, which is a declaration of rabbinic authority. Although the Talmud contains a good deal of wisdom and godly teaching, one of the major goals of its authors was to keep the Jew from believing in Messiah Jesus. It distorts many of the Messianic interpretations of the Jewish Scriptures. There is clear evidence that *before* Jesus came to earth, the Jewish people were expecting a Messiah and interpreted the Messianic prophecies without bias.

Today, the rabbis claim the Talmud, or Oral Law,

came from God at the same time the Written Law was given to Moses on Mount Sinai. This is not true. Even in the first century, Jewish leaders did not claim rabbinic law came from Sinai. Instead they spoke of "oral traditions." The Jewish Bible, the Dead Sea Scrolls, and the Jewish historian Josephus (A.D. 93) do not even mention an oral law.

The method of interpreting Scripture employed by Akiba and his followers rejected the rules of grammar and plain logic. Author Dan Gruber writes, "Sometimes the Rabbis were unable to read their teachings into the Scriptures by any means. So they simply annulled the decrees of Torah."[2]

They proclaimed rabbinic authority took precedence over the Scriptures.[3] The Talmud states, "My son, take heed of the words of the Scribes more than the words of the Torah."[4] Akiba's objective was to bring the Jewish people under the rule of the rabbis.

The Talmud even says that if a voice from heaven contradicts the majority of the rabbis, the rabbis are correct.[5] In other words, nobody is allowed to contradict the authority of the rabbis, not even God! Is it any wonder, then, that between persecution from the church and the rabbinic conspiracy, Jewish people know nothing about Jesus?

While there was a sect of Judaism that created this new rabbinic form, it is important to understand that at the time of Jesus' First Coming there were *three* main sects within Judaism: Pharisees, Sadducees, and Essenes. These three disagreed on the core theological issues of Judaism.

Today we are most familiar with the view of the
Pharisees. They believed God had no triune nature
and that the Word of God consisted of both the Old
Covenant Scriptures (Tenach) and the oral traditions.
They were looking for a Messiah who would initiate
true peace and rule the world. The Pharisees are the
fathers of modern-day Rabbinic Judaism.

The *Sadducees* only accepted the first five books of
the Old Testament (Torah) as legal and binding. They
rejected the resurrection of the dead and the existence
of angels. Their focus was more on political matters
rather than religious.

The *Essenes* were the largest Jewish sect during Jesus'
earthly ministry. Most of the first Jewish followers of
Jesus came from this sect. Why? The Dead Sea Scrolls
tell us the Essenes believed in the triune nature of God.
They accepted the entire Tenach (Old Covenant) as
true, but rejected the Oral Law. The Essenes expected
the appearance of an atoning Messiah. Messianic Jewish author Dr. Robert Fischer notes, "It was only the
Essenes who had a clear understanding of Mashiyach's
[Messiah's] absolute Divinity, precise sacrificial purpose, Davidic lineage and eschatological timing."[6] By
understanding the Essenes, we see that Jesus the Messiah was the fulfillment of their expectations, not the
founder of a new Gentile religion.

WHO IS THE MESSIAH?

In modern times, the rabbis have missed two of the
most significant events to happen to the Jewish people

in the last two thousand years. Messianic Jewish author Ron Cantor notes that many rabbis initially opposed the creation of Israel as a modern Jewish nation. "Many of the rabbis of Jerusalem were actually siding with the Arabs to keep this from happening. They believed only the Messiah could set up a Jewish state."[7] They also vehemently opposed Eliezer Ben Yehuda's plans to restore Hebrew as the national language of the Jewish people in the late 1800s.

Cantor notes, "If it was so clear to the rabbis that both the Jewish state and the Hebrew language were the dreams of false prophets and yet they were wrong, it is possible that they also missed it on the single most important issue in Judaism—the Messiah!"[8]

DOES ISAIAH 53 SPEAK OF JESUS?

Although Isaiah 53 is in the accepted Jewish Scriptures (Tenach), it is not part of the regular synagogue readings. Isaiah recorded this prophecy seven centuries before Jesus was born. Because it is not read in the synagogues, the Jewish people miss the most graphic description of Jesus in the Jewish Scriptures.

When I share this passage with rabbis, some say they are not holy enough and must read what the rabbis in the past had to say about it. But they don't go back far enough. They only consult the rabbis after Jesus—the ones who distorted the Messianic Scriptures. The rabbis before Jesus were not prejudiced and saw the Messianic significance of this passage.[9] Others insult my intelligence by saying the prophet is speaking of Israel rather than Jesus. Yet, Isaiah 53:8–9 says that the One who would die for the sins of the world would have no sin of His own. This could not be Israel. There are numerous places in Scripture where the prophets point out Israel's sins. No nation is sinless before God.

When my own Orthodox Jewish father read Isaiah 53, he knew immediately that the prophet was describing Jesus—despite being taught all his life that Jesus was *not* the Jewish Messiah.

THINK FOR YOURSELF

Jeremiah predicted a new covenant that would wipe away sins and allow us to know (have intimacy with) God (Jer. 31:31–34). The Jewish Scriptures tell us that the Messiah would be born in Bethlehem (Mic. 5:2 in some translations, Mic. 5:1). He would be raised from the dead (Ps. 16:10). Daniel 9:26 makes it clear that He would die before the second temple was destroyed. Since it was destroyed in A.D. 70, He had to come, die, and be resurrected before that time! And Isaiah 11:10 tells us that the Gentiles will follow the Jewish Messiah.

What other person do you know of who was born in Bethlehem, who was followed by the Gentiles, who was sacrificed for our sins before the destruction of the second temple, and who was raised from the dead?

Please take a moment to read the prophecies about the Messiah in Appendix C and to have your own God encounter.

CHAPTER 3

Who Is Israel?

My friend the late Dr. Derek Prince wrote, "Almost limitless misunderstanding, ignorance and distortion have pervaded the church for many centuries concerning the identity of Israel. This seems extraordinary to me because the statements in the Bible regarding Israel are so clear. Nevertheless, the minds of multitudes of Christians seem to be clouded in regard to the application of the name Israel."[1] Dr. Prince also said that a Christian who has no particular love for the Jew and Israel is "deficient" and "incomplete."[2]

So, who is Israel? Did Jews forfeit their birthright to the Christians, just as Esau did to Jacob? Has the Christian church replaced the Jews in God's sight? Not hardly. This erroneous theology known as "Replacement Theology" is blinding many to the truth.

Replacement Theology is a teaching that says the church has replaced Israel in God's eyes and inherited its blessings while the Jews are cursed. Under this logic, Scripture is interpreted by replacing references to Israel with the words, "the church." A reading of Romans 9–11 will demonstrate to us the need to *replace* Replacement Theology. God's promises to the Jewish people are *irrevocable*. (See Appendix A for a more complete discussion of Replacement Theology.)

Some Gentile believers say, "I feel Jewish. I have such a love for Jewish people and Jewish festivals, I must have Jewish blood." Your reaction is normal. After all, in a spiritual sense, you have the blood of Jesus, the greatest Jew who ever lived, flowing through your veins! If you *did not* have a supernatural love for the Jew and Israel, I would question whether you know Jesus. However, your supernatural love for God's people does not make you a *physical* Jew.

One Gentile Christian I know thinks she is an Israelite or an "Ephraimite" because she *might* have had one ancestor over the past two thousand years who was of the lost tribes of Israel. She bases her belief on allegorical interpretations of Scripture rather than the literal.

But we have no right to spiritualize God's Word if our interpretation contradicts the literal meaning.

Let's start with simple definitions. The word *Hebrew* was first used to identify Abram's (Abraham's) family (Gen. 14:13). It was Abraham's grandson Jacob who was first called "Israel" after he wrestled with God (Gen.

32:28). Later, the nation of Israel was divided into two sections, the southern tribes of Judah and Benjamin, and the ten northern tribes. A "Jew" is literally a *physical* descendant from the tribe of Judah. An "Israelite" is a *physical* descendant from the ten northern tribes. However, in Ezekiel 37:16, God calls Judah and Ephraim (the ten northern tribes) "Israel." Today the term *Jew* is used to identify all those who are the physical seed of Abraham through his son Isaac. Paul, who was from the tribe of Benjamin, called himself a Jew, an Israelite, and a Hebrew (Phil. 3:5, Acts 21:39, and Rom. 11:1), proving all three terms are used interchangeably.

ARE YOU JEALOUS?

Why do so many Christians believe they have replaced Israel? Why do so many Gentile believers want to be Jewish or to call themselves Israel or Ephraim?[3] Why do they need to be the physical seed of Abraham when they are *the spiritual seed* of Abraham through Jesus? Why would they want to miss their destiny? Jews need Gentile believers, and Gentile believers need Jews.

Ruth understood this interdependent relationship. If this Gentile had not attached herself to Naomi the Jew, she would have never met Boaz, also a Jew. The fruit of this marriage produced Obed, the grandfather of King David. Jesus was a descendant of King David.

If Esther, the Jew, did not marry King Ahasuerus, the Gentile, the Jewish people would have perished. When the Jews were spared, it sparked a revival among the Gentiles. The Book of Esther says many became Jews (Esther 8:17).

There will be no One New Man without the Jew and the Gentile fulfilling their destinies. In the Spirit, there is no difference between Jew and Gentile any more than there is a difference in the Spirit between male and female (Gal. 3:28). Yet, a Jew has a unique physical calling just as men and women have different physical callings. The Jewish person, whether he knows it or not, is called by God to live in the land of Israel. The Spirit of God will tell the Jewish believer when to move—although some will be martyrs in the nations. For Jewish nonbelievers, the catalyst to relocate to Israel will be persecution. Beyond living in Israel, Jewish people have a unique mandate and anointing to proclaim the gospel to the Gentiles. Watch the Scriptures finally being fulfilled when the Word of the Lord is proclaimed from Israel to the nations (Isa. 2:3).

The Gentile believer also has a unique purpose. This high calling is being accelerated in these last days. Salvation has come to the Gentile to evangelize the Jews (Rom. 11:11). In other words, the Gentile believer has a biblical mandate and anointing to proclaim the gospel to the Jews. We need each other. And when we come together, the merger of these two anointings will cause the dead religious church to explode with the glory of God.

Each group envies what the other one has: the Jew longs for signs and miracles. The Gentiles long for the Father's inheritance. I compare the jealousy between

Jews and Gentiles to the parable of the prodigal son. You may have heard other applications of this parable, but this is what God has shown me.

The younger son is a type of the Jewish people. The older son is a type of the Gentile church. When the younger son returned home, the father (a type of Father God) held a great celebration with food, music, and dancing. The older brother was jealous. Luke 15:28 says that he "was angry [with deep-seated wrath] and resolved not to go in" (AMP). The older brother did not understand that the father longed to be reconciled to the younger brother.

Many Gentiles do not understand the One New Man. They do not realize that the Jew must be grafted into the body of Messiah in order to have the wedding supper of the Lamb (the heavenly feast enjoyed by the Messiah and His bride, the church). The older brother cannot comprehend the truth expressed by Jesus that He would not return until the Jewish people were restored to the Father (Matt. 23:39). He could not see that by being in the seed of Abraham, everything the Father had was already his (Luke 15:31).

When the Jew comes back to the Father, God will bring a new type of music and dancing into the church. Religious Gentile Christians, who are stuck in their traditions, will be angry over this new wave of worship and will refuse to participate.

After two thousand years of living out in the world, we Jewish believers have a lot of rough edges. Gentile Christians (older brothers) have a sweetness about them because of generations of knowing the Messiah. As

Jewish believers, we desperately need to be embraced by our older brothers.

There is one body. The body of Messiah is not Messianic Jewish and Gentile Christian. It is not two streams having joint meetings. When God sees the body, He does not see Jew and Gentile, male or female, but He sees His Son, Jesus. He is the One New Man, the King of the Jews!

ARE WE REALLY RELATED?

When a Christian looks at a Jew, he thinks, *I don't see anything Christian about you.* And when a Jew looks at a Christian, he thinks, *I don't see anything Jewish about you.* The rabbis say, "You can't be Jewish and believe in Jesus." Many Christians feel the same way.

How did the Jewish Messiah who was prophesied by the Jewish prophets in the Jewish Scriptures and who came "only" to the Jewish people (Matt. 15:24) become so Gentile? Are we related?

The first followers of Jesus were Jewish. The only Bible they had was the Jewish Scriptures. The first church followed the biblical festivals, worshiped in the traditional synagogues, and was a sect within Judaism that believed Jesus was the Jewish Messiah.

The big controversy at the Jerusalem Council meeting in Acts 15:6–21 was over whether Gentiles had to become Jews to be saved. They do not. Today the big question is whether a Jew has to become a Gentile to be saved, which is not true.

THE JEW FIRST

The early church reached out to the Jew first. I call this the "Law of Evangelism," which I will discuss in more detail in chapter eight. God began this pattern by going to the first Jew, Abraham, to reach all the families on earth (Gen. 12:3). Jesus instructed His first followers to go only "to the lost sheep of the house of Israel" (Matt. 10:5–6). Paul said in Romans 1:16, "the gospel...is...for the Jew first...." Although Paul was the apostle to the Gentiles, he always went to the Jew first.

As the early church spread into the non-Jewish world, it took on a more Gentile culture. Eventually, Gentiles outnumbered Jewish believers, and then the Jewish roots of the church were removed.

CHECKMATE OF THE DEVIL

The restoration of the Jewish people to the body of Messiah is the key for worldwide revival. At the Jerusalem Council meeting in Acts 15, James quoted the prophet Amos: "I will...rebuild the tabernacle of David...so that the rest of mankind may seek the LORD, even all the Gentiles who are called by My name..." (vv. 16–17). The word *tabernacle* can be translated "house" or "family." What is Amos saying? When the family of David (the Jewish people) are restored (grafted back into their own olive tree), there will be revival among the Gentiles, and not just any revival. Amos goes on to compare it to land producing crops so quickly that "the plowman shall overtake the reaper" (Amos 9:13).

There has never been a time like this in history. The harvest of souls will be so great that church buildings will not be able to contain it.

Now you can understand the heart of God at this moment in history. Now you can see why so many Gentile Christians are interested in the Jewish roots of their faith. The Spirit of God is speaking this revelation to the church worldwide. When the Jew is saved, not only will it open a supernatural door for large numbers of Gentiles to be saved, but it will also be the checkmate of the devil—the return of Jesus (Matt. 23:39).

In order for the Jewish people to want what we (the church) have, we must restore three key ingredients. The first is true intimacy with God. All services and ministry will flow out of this intimacy as opposed to tradition. The second key is for even the believer with the smallest amount of faith to move in the supernatural love and miracle-working power of God. The third key ingredient will be joyous celebrations of the biblical feasts. Adam enjoyed pure fellowship with God before sin brought separation and death. The second Adam, Jesus, came to restore that which was lost. God desires the same intimacy with us that He had with Adam before the Fall. He has even set appointments to meet with us.

"MY APPOINTMENTS"

God said in Leviticus 23:2, "The *feasts* of the LORD, which you shall proclaim to be holy *convocations*, these are *My feasts*" (emphasis added). In Hebrew, the word translated "feasts" means "appointments," and the word translated "convocations" means "rehearsals." These appointments (feasts) with God are not only Jewish appointments, not only biblical appointments, but also God calls them "*My* appointments!"

There are seven specific appointments when God promises to meet with us. The first three were rehearsals of His First Coming and the outpouring of the Holy Spirit. I believe the next three are rehearsals of His Second Coming. And the seventh, the Sabbath (*Shabbat*), is a rehearsal of the millennial rule of Jesus on earth.

If you had attended a dress rehearsal (convocation) of His First Coming before it happened, you would not have missed it. The same is true today. Celebrating the rehearsals (convocations) will help you prepare for His return.

In John's Gospel, 660 of the 879 verses are directly related to events occurring at the feasts. How can you understand the Gospels unless you understand the feasts?

Never let a religious spirit put you under bondage with these rehearsals. Observance is not a matter of righteousness or salvation, but blessings. Isaiah 58:13–14 says those who observe the Sabbath are promised to be so blessed that they will "ride on the high hills of the earth."

God tells us that when we bless the Jewish people we will be blessed in return (Gen. 12:3). What greater way to do this than by inviting Jewish people to great celebrations where God promises in writing to meet with us? The reason God's glory will be released is because we will have such intimacy with Him and we will yield completely to His Spirit. Every year our celebration of the festivals will be different. We will lay down our agenda for God's.

PREPARE THE WAY

"The Jews require a sign [or miracle]" (1 Cor. 1:22, KJV). When we move into these God-appointed celebrations with Holy Spirit revelation and glory, miracles will take place, which will invoke jealousy in the Jew. Then the prayer of Jesus in John 17:21–22 will finally be answered. He prayed that the only people groups at the time—Jews and Gentiles—would be one. The Jews will be grafted back into the Olive Tree, and Jesus says this combination will cause the world to believe.

Jesus is not returning for a fractured, powerless bride. As the body of Messiah is restored, we will do the same works as Jesus and even greater. This supernatural unity of Jew and Gentile will prepare the way for the Lord. When the pattern is right, the glory will come down!

CHAPTER 4

When the Pattern Is Right...

I am a Jew. Although as I was growing up I attended a traditional synagogue, it never dawned on me that I could know God personally. The stories about Moses, Noah, and Abraham belonged to another era. God seemed to be a million miles away—not relevant to my life. Even the most devout, older men in the synagogue were more interested in the ritualistic prayers and fellowship with their friends than having an intimate relationship with God.

Today, most Jewish people are more secular than religious. When I was young, Jews at least went to the synagogue on high holidays like Rosh Hashanah and Yom Kippur. Now the majority of my people do not attend services at all.

When I encountered Jesus at the age of thirty,

everything in my world changed. I not only knew God was real, but I now knew Him personally. My biggest shock was to discover that Christians, for the most part, act like most Jews. They know about God. They believe in Him. They think they will probably go to heaven. Yet some have greater intimacy with their denomination than with God. Others attend church merely for the social interaction. These Sunday and "high-holiday" (Easter and Christmas) Christians compartmentalize God to their convenience. They treat Jesus more as their Servant than their Lord. They surrender Sunday mornings—not their lives.

Many churches have evolved into nothing more than human warehouses. Members are made to feel as if they are acceptable to God without repentance of sin. Their church experience is as spectators who never fulfill their destinies in God. Tragically, many do not even have a personal relationship with Jesus.

Over the years I began to see that even some of the better churches are filled with religious tradition. The pastors appear to be more concerned with the offering, announcements, a full sermon, and ending on time rather than yielding to the leading of the Holy Spirit.

The more I hungered for greater intimacy with God, the more dissatisfied I became. Then God led me into a study of the history of the early church. The blinders of tradition fell from my eyes. I began to see the Scriptures in a whole new light.

Now I understand why there are so few miracles, even in believing, Spirit-filled churches. Now I know why so few believers fulfill their destiny in God. Now

I know why the system forces the services to be man-controlled rather than God-controlled. Now I know why there is so little compassion for the souls of men and for the poor. Now I know why the same sins of secular society pervade the church. Now I know how we have grieved the Holy Spirit through ignorance, compromise, tradition, and the fear of man. Now I know why the glory under Moses was greater than our best churches today.

God has been waiting for a generation of believers to follow the cloud of His presence just as the Israelites followed the cloud in the wilderness. The cloud is moving. Will you follow the cloud to glory, or will you remain stuck in your old ways?

Only a few of the older believers will enter this new land. The rest will observe it from afar. I am hungry for more. How about you?

Just as God had a specific plan for the Israelites to enter the Promised Land, He also instructed them on how to enter His glory. God said to Moses, "See that you make all things according to the *pattern...*" (Heb. 8:5, emphasis added). The pattern is God's bridge to intimacy. When the pattern is right, the glory explodes.

Notice I did not say "formula," but "pattern." Man wants to place God in a box, which is why we have so many religions and denominations. God is too big to be limited by our attempts to define Him. We cannot reduce His pattern to a "formula."

That is what many did with a popular teaching about standing on God's Word for healing. Although many were healed and there is great truth in that teaching, for some the healing did not manifest. Those who knew God by the formula were quickly offended and abandoned their belief in healing. Some lost their faith in God altogether. But those who had genuine faith in God used that disappointment to draw closer to Him. The biblical pattern always leads to greater intimacy with God.

It also leads to unity between Jew and Gentile. I believe that today God is calling us to a new level in which both Jewish and Gentile believers will come together as One New Man—yielded to His Spirit and walking in power.

"For I am about to do a brand-new thing. See, I have already begun!" (Isa. 43:19, NLT).

FIRST THE NATURAL, THEN THE SPIRITUAL

God's pattern that defines the relationship between the church and the Jewish people is explained in 1 Corinthians 15:46: "The spiritual is not first, but the natural, and afterward the spiritual." First, God acts with His natural "witness" people, Israel, then He acts with His spiritual people, the church. His true church is made up of those who genuinely believe in Jesus as Savior and Lord. The church and Israel are *mishpochah*, which is Hebrew for "family." Whatever happens to Israel dramatically affects the restoration of the church.

For example, in 1897 Theodor Herzl convened the first Zionist Congress in Basel, Switzerland, to investigate the formation of a Jewish homeland. The beginning of the restoration of the land was followed by the beginning of the restoration of the manifest presence of the Holy Spirit back to the church. On New Year's Eve 1900, at a Bible school in Topeka, Kansas, a thirty-year-old student named Agnes Ozman began to speak in tongues—the start of the Pentecostal Revival. Several days later, Charles Parham and other students also received the baptism of the Holy Spirit with the gift of speaking in tongues. After William Seymour sat under Parham's teaching, he took this fire to a home prayer meeting in Los Angeles that birthed the world-famous Azusa Street Revival.

Around the time when Israel became a nation in 1948, God responded by bringing the healing revival to the United States. Over one hundred evangelists such as Oral Roberts, Kathryn Kuhlman, T. L. Osborn, and Kenneth Hagin began tremendous healing ministries. Billy Graham's ministry started then also.

In 1967 Israel regained possession of Jerusalem for the first time since the temple was destroyed. That same year the Catholic Charismatic movement started. It went on to impact Christians from all denominations. The late 1960s also gave birth to the "Jesus Movement" by which thousands of hippies were swept into the kingdom of God.

Around the time of the Yom Kippur War in 1973, there was a revival among Jewish people resulting in the modern-day Messianic Jewish movement.

WHAT'S NEXT?

If you want to know what will be the next move of God on the church, then watch Israel. Because of sin, God scattered the Jewish people to the four corners of the earth. But in the last days He promises to restore them back to Israel. (See Ezekiel 37:21.)

In the Old Covenant, the nation of Israel was a "divided" land. The northern kingdom was called "Israel," and the southern kingdom, "Judah." Judah and Israel fought with each other. God promises to restore these two kingdoms and return them to their land. They will be "one" nation under one King:

> And I will make them one nation in the land, on the mountains of Israel; and one king shall be king over them all; they shall no longer be two nations, nor shall they ever be divided into two kingdoms again.
>
> —EZEKIEL 37:22

Today we are seeing these scriptures fulfilled before our eyes. Israel is a nation again, and the Jews are returning to Israel in record numbers. A sign of the hastening of the prophetic time clock is when the Jews from the "north" of Israel (former Soviet Union) return to the land. Jeremiah 16:14–16 says once this happens, Jews from the entire world will return to Israel.

We are also beginning to see the spiritual fulfillment of this prophecy. The two covenant peoples of God, Jews and Christians, who have fought with each other will unite under one King—Jesus. This will cause a spiritual explosion in the church.

The devil's worst nightmare will come to pass when the sleeping giant, the church, finally realizes that the underlying purpose for the current outpourings of the Holy Spirit is to equip believers with power to evangelize the Jew. When the Jewish people join with the Gentiles to form One New Man, it will trigger a major release of power to evangelize the world! But before the church can enter this glorious future, it must first overcome its anti-Semitic past.

PART 2
THE CHANGEOVER

So a curse without cause shall not alight.
—PROVERBS 26:2

CHAPTER 5

Christian?

od has a marvelous plan for bringing about the unity of the Jew and the Gentile in Messiah Jesus. The apostle Paul writes, "To provoke [the Jews] to jealousy, salvation has come to the Gentiles" (Rom. 11:11). God wants to use Gentiles to bring the Jewish people back into the body of Messiah.

Somehow that truth has gotten lost. To provoke the Jew to jealousy means to demonstrate supernatural peace, healing, strong family relationships, and love that only comes from intimacy with God. It means causing the Jew to want what Gentile believers have.

Instead of driving the Jewish people to jealousy, the Christian church has simply driven them away. Although there are believers who have given their lives for the Jews,[1] some of the most anti-Jewish people in

the last two thousand years have been those who have
called themselves Christians. Through the centuries,
accusations and statements by church leaders against
the Jews have led to a vicious form of "Christian" anti-
Semitism. Here are a few examples:[2]

- Justin Martyr (d. A.D. 167) was one of the
  first to accuse the Jews of inciting to kill
  Christians.

- Origen (d. A.D. 254) accused Jews of plotting
  in their meetings to murder Christians.

- Eusebius (c. A.D. 300) alleged that Jews, each
  year at the holiday of Purim, engaged in cer-
  emonial killing of Christian children.

- St. Hilary of Poitiers (d. A.D. 367) said that
  the Jews were a perverse people, forever
  accursed by God.

- St. Ephraem (d. A.D. 373) wrote many of the
  early church hymns, some of which maligned
  Jews, even to the point of calling the Jewish
  synagogues "whore houses."

- St. John Chrysostom (A.D. 344–407) said that
  there could never be expiation for the Jews
  and that God had always hated them. He said
  it was "incumbent" upon all Christians to hate
  the Jews; they were assassins of Christ, and
  worshipers of the devil.
     In one of his homilies, Chrysostom stated:
  "The synagogue is worse than a brothel....It

is a den of scoundrels and the repair of wild beasts...the temple of demons devoted to idolatrous cults...the refuge of brigands and debauchees, and the cavern of devils."[3]

- St. Cyril (d. A.D. 444) gave the Jews within his jurisdiction the choice of conversion, exile, or stoning.

- St. Jerome (d. A.D. 420), translator of the Latin Vulgate, "proved" that Jews are incapable of understanding the Scriptures and said they should be severely persecuted until they confess the "true faith."

- St. Augustine (d. A.D. 430) said the true image of the Jew was Judas Iscariot, forever guilty and spiritually ignorant. St. Augustine decided that Jews, for their own good and the good of society, must be relegated to the position of slaves. This theme was later picked up by St. Thomas Aquinas (d. A.D. 1274), who demanded that Jews be called to perpetual servitude.

  According to Professor F. E. Talmage, St. Augustine believed that "because of their sin against Christ, the Jews rightly deserved death. Yet, as with Cain who murdered the just Abel, they are not to die....For they are doomed to wander the earth....the 'witnesses of their iniquity and of our truth,' the living proof of Christianity."[4]

- The Crusaders (A.D. 1099) herded Jews into
  the Great Synagogue in Jerusalem. When
  they were securely inside the locked doors, the
  synagogue was set on fire. And the misguided
  Crusaders, with the lies of perverted sermons
  fresh in their ears, sang as they marched
  around the blaze, "Christ, we adore Thee."

- Martin Luther (c. A.D. 1544) said the Jews
  should not merely be slaves, but slaves of
  slaves and that they might not even come
  into contact with Christians. In his Schem
  Hamphoras, he said the Jews were ritual mur-
  derers and poisoners of wells. He called for all
  Talmuds and synagogues to be destroyed.

  In his Von den Juden und Iren Luegen
  (1543), Luther wrote: "What then shall we
  Christians do with this damned, rejected
  race of Jews? Since they live among us and
  we know about their lying and blasphemy
  and cursing, we cannot tolerate them if we
  do not wish to share in their lies, curses, and
  blasphemy.... We must prayerfully and rever-
  entially practice a merciful severity."[5]

  Encyclopaedia Judaica comments on Luther's
  statements: "Short of the Auschwitz oven and
  extermination, the whole Nazi Holocaust
  is pre-outlined here."[6] Indeed, Adolph
  Hitler wrote in Mein Kampf, "Hence today I
  believe that I am acting in accordance with
  the Almighty Creator: by defending myself
  against the Jew, I am fighting for the work of
  the Lord."[7]

Speaking as part of the church, we need a restoration miracle. Only God can restore the damage between the church and the Jewish people. Repentance is the first step. We may not have been knowingly anti-Semitic, but as members of His body, we must repent for the sins of the whole church. Daniel did not rebel against God, but he repented on behalf of Israel. Some feel we should not talk of this sad history. Then how can we ever repent and get clean?[8] The church must be rid of this horrible sin. Without holiness, we will not see God (Heb. 12:14).

ALL ISRAEL WILL BE SAVED

Repentance will prepare the way for a great Jewish revival. God says, "For I do not desire, brethren, that you should be ignorant of this mystery...blindness in part has happened to Israel until the fullness [maturity] of the Gentiles has come in. And so all Israel will be saved" (Rom. 11:25–26). In other words, as the Gentiles who believe in Jesus become spiritually mature, the Jewish people will become open to the gospel. Step one toward maturity involves repentance.

Thank God for the Passover Lamb who takes away the sins of the whole world!

CHAPTER 6

The Constantine Conspiracy

Can a believer be under a curse for the anti-Semitic attitudes of his ancestors? Just ask John Doe.* While serving in the U.S. armed forces, John had a life-changing visitation from God that lasted for three days. The Lord revealed to him that he was Jewish. John later discovered that his grandfather had changed his last name when he immigrated to America in order to hide his Jewish identity.

Then God told John he was under a family curse for denying his Jewish heritage and that the curse had to be broken. After he prayed to break the curse, John was flooded with revelation and blessings.

God says He will bless those who bless the Jewish people and curse those who curse them (Gen. 12:3).

*Fictitious name

MIXTURE IN GOD'S HOUSE

Could the church be under a family curse as John was? Has the church denied its Jewish heritage? Yes. As we saw in the previous chapter, anti-Semitism has been a prominent part of church history for centuries. This was not an "accident." It was part of a deliberate plan to separate the church from anything Jewish. Let's call it for what it was—a conspiracy.

The first church was Jewish. If a Gentile wanted to follow the Messiah, he had to convert to Judaism. Then Peter had a revelation that Gentiles did not have to become Jews to be saved (Acts 10). The Jerusalem Council meeting determined that Gentiles did not have to be circumcised. There were only four easily followed requirements. They were to "abstain from things polluted by idols, from sexual immorality, from things strangled, and from blood" (Acts 15:20). This opened the door to widespread church growth among the Gentiles. So many Gentiles were saved that the Jewish believers became a minority.

The first Jewish followers of Jesus were called "Nazarenes" (part of the Essenes sect of Judaism discussed in chapter two). They practiced traditional Judaism and were widely accepted by non-believing Jews. Early in the second century their numbers reached 400,000.[1] In the Book of Acts, the early church fathers said to Paul: "You see, brother, how many myriads [tens of thousands] of Jews there are who have believed, and they are all zealous for the law" (Acts 21:20).

The Nazarenes' acceptance by traditional Jews came

to a halt in A.D. 135 when Rabbi Akiba declared that Bar Kochba was the Jewish Messiah. His followers hoped he would lead them to victory over the Romans. The Nazarenes refused to fight because they believed Jesus was the true Messiah rather than Bar Kochba. They were branded traitors, not because they believed in Jesus, but because they would not join Bar Kochba's armed struggle. Bar Kochba and his followers were quickly slaughtered by the Romans. Afterward, Jews were banned from Jerusalem.

History shows that as the center of the Christian faith moved from Jerusalem to Rome, it became increasingly Hellenized, adopting pagan customs and philosophies rather than the God-ordained practices and beliefs of the Bible. At the same time Christianity became increasingly anti-Jewish.

In the early fourth century (A.D. 306–337), Constantine, a Roman emperor, came into power. He was a master politician. He tried to attract heathens to Christianity by modifying pagan customs and festivals and giving them Christian meanings, which would still allow the Christians to keep their traditions. The group he didn't like was the Jews since they had rebelled against Rome. And the church was more than willing to follow Constantine's lead in order to avoid persecution. Christians were prohibited from worshiping on Saturday or observing Passover, upon the threat of excommunication or worse.

Constantine expressed the anti-Judaic sentiments of the bishops of the Christian world when he wrote: "Let us therefore have nothing in common with this odious people, the Jews, for we have received from our Savior a different way.... Strive and pray continually that the purity of your souls may not be sullied by fellowship with the customs of these most wicked men.... All should unite in desiring that which sound reason appears to demand in avoiding all participation in the perjured conduct of the Jews."[2]

In A.D. 196, without the presence of Jewish believers, a church council meeting in Caesarea changed the celebration of Jesus' resurrection from the third day of Passover [Firstfruits] (Lev. 23:9–11; 1 Cor. 15:4, 20–23) to Sunday, during the feast of the pagan fertility goddess, Ishtar. In the fourth century, the Council of Nicea (headed by the Roman Emperor Constantine) made the change official. The decision was based on the premise that it was not proper for the church in her celebrations to be connected with "the cursed Jewish nation" that crucified Him.[3]

Today, the holiday is known as Easter (from Ishtar). Have you ever wondered why we have Easter bunnies and eggs? These are vestiges of Ishtar worship.

TOO COLD

Another major change started early in church history was the celebration of Christmas. Today it is the most hallowed religious holiday next to Easter. But was Jesus born on December 25? According to Luke 2:8, we know He was not. Shepherds would not have been out in the field watching their flocks *at night* in

Bethlehem in December (winter season) because it would have been too cold.

It makes more sense that Jesus was born about the time of Sukkot (Feast of Tabernacles). This feast is referred to as "the Season of Our Joy." What greater joy than for Messiah to tabernacle—or dwell—with man?

Scripture tells us that the law, which includes biblical festivals, is a "shadow of the good things to come" (Heb. 10:1). Sukkot foreshadows the dwelling of God with man. "And the Word became flesh and *dwelt* [tabernacled] among us" (John 1:14, emphasis added). The Feast of Tabernacles provides a much better picture of Jesus than Christmas.

So where did the idea of celebrating the birth of Jesus on December 25 originate? Babylonian pagans believed the sun was god. The winter solstice began on December 21 and represented the death of the sun. By December 25, the sun's climb in the sky and a wild celebration of its "rebirth" took place. This rebirth celebration was in honor of the incarnation of the sun god and his mother, the "queen of heaven." To draw pagans into Christianity, the Roman Catholic Church proclaimed December 25 to be the birthday of the Messiah, although this is not mentioned in Scripture. The festival was called "Christ's Masse" and was later shortened to *Christmas*.[4] The early Puritans knew this history and did not celebrate Christmas.[5]

WHATEVER HAPPENED TO THE SABBATH?

Another reform by the Council of Nicea "institutional-ized" the change of the day of Christian worship from Saturday to Sunday. As with Easter, the change had actually started much earlier. In fact, by the middle of the second century, Sunday, the day devoted to the sun god, had largely replaced Saturday, the day devoted to the one true God.

The Sabbath was the first element of Creation that God sanctified, or set apart, in remembrance of His creative power. That God rested on the Sabbath day is a biblical fact. Nevertheless, the change was made and justified by the church leaders, and not initially on the basis of the Resurrection. The primary rationale for the observance of Sunday was to commemorate the first day of Creation. The resurrection of Jesus was only a secondary issue.

Many of the church leaders who originally changed the Sabbath day were anti-Semitic. Tertullian thought that God had always hated the Sabbath.[6] The Epistle of Barnabas (apocryphal literature from the first century A.D.) denies altogether that God had ever given the Sabbath as a commandment to be kept. Justin Martyr (d. A.D. 167) considered the Sabbath to be a highly deserved curse on the Jewish people.

Martyr lectured Trypho the Jew by saying, "It was by reason of your sins and the sins of your Fathers that, among other precepts, God imposed upon you the observance of the Sabbath as a mark." This "mark" was to "single them out for the punishment they so well deserved for their infidelities."[7]

Instead of recognizing that "the Sabbath was made for man" (Mark 2:27), the Sabbath was seen as part of the curse of the law upon that hated and despised race—the Jews. The post-apostolic church instituted another day of worship to separate themselves from all things Jewish. This anti-Judaism was reflected in the Replacement Theology of the early writers of the Hellenized church. (See Appendix A for a more complete discussion of Replacement Theology.)

WHERE'S THE POWER?

It is no coincidence that when the Jewish biblical heritage of the church was replaced with paganism, intimacy with God was watered down. The church went from everyone doing the works of Jesus to professional clergy leading a congregation of spectators. The supernatural power of God was replaced with the politics and traditions of men.[8] Jesus warned against this when He rebuked the religious leaders of His day for "making the word of God no effect through your tradition" (Mark 7:13).

When the church walked away from its biblical Jewish roots, it abandoned God's pattern. The original "church split" was the division between Jew and Gentile. When the Jewish believers and Gentile believers come together in Jesus, we will break the curse off of the church and clear the way for widespread revival.

CHAPTER 7

Biblical Festivals— Blessing or Bondage?

God says that at the time of the full maturity of the Gentiles, the Jewish people will be grafted back into their *own* olive tree (Rom. 11:24–25). Isn't it time the body of Messiah become mature and start to look like the Jewish olive tree?

The biggest lie the devil tells Jewish people is that they can't be Jewish and believe in Jesus. By hiding its Jewish roots, the church has reinforced this lie. Now is the time for Jewish believers and Christians alike to see Christianity's Jewish connection and celebrate this union. Part of the church's heritage is to observe the biblical festivals as God meant for them to be observed. As a means of reinforcing the unity of the two streams into one, I will refer to Jesus by His Hebrew name, Yeshua, for the remainder of the book.

UNDER THE LAW?

The first church observed all the biblical festivals. During the Millennium (the thousand-year reign of Yeshua on earth) we will observe the Sabbath (Isa. 66:23), the Feast of Tabernacles (Zech. 14:16–17), Rosh Hashanah (Feast of Trumpets), the Passover, and the Feast of Unleavened Bread (Ezek. 45:20–21). Why have we put these celebrations "on hold" for centuries?

One reason is that many resist anything that appears to put them "under the law." Paul makes it clear that we are not justified by the law (Rom. 3:20; Eph. 2:8–9). Does this mean the law has no value? Should we disregard such laws as the Ten Commandments? Of course not. Paul proclaimed, "Therefore the law is holy, and the commandment holy and just and good" (Rom. 7:12).

Yeshua explained this paradox in Matthew 5:18: "Till heaven and earth pass away, one jot or one tittle will by no means pass from the law till all is fulfilled." The key word in this passage is *fulfilled*. This word is best understood by reversing the syllables of "fulfilled" to "filled-full." Yeshua is the "full" meaning of the law. He did not come to eliminate the law but to enable us to "fill it full" of its true meaning.

Yeshua was never upset with the Torah (first five books of the Bible). He said, "Do not think that I came to destroy the Law [Torah] or the Prophets. I did not come to destroy but to *fulfill*" (Matt. 5:17, emphasis added). What He did object to were the ways in which the rabbis would cleverly overrule many portions of the Torah. Yeshua asked, "Why do you also transgress the commandment of God because of your tradition?" (Matt. 15:3).

Before you conclude that I am advocating a new form of bondage or legalism, please let's get one thing straight. Celebrating the Jewish biblical feasts has nothing to do with obtaining salvation or righteousness. This was the mistake of the Judaizers in the Book of Galatians. It is only through repentance of our sins and the blood of Yeshua that we are saved. Nothing more is needed. However, observing the festivals does bring blessing and leads to greater intimacy with God.

APPOINTED TIMES

So what should be our attitude toward the biblical feasts? The Hebrew word for "feasts" is *mo'ed*, which means "appointed times." Leviticus 23:2 makes it clear that these are not only Jewish feasts, but they are *God's* feasts. In other words, these are God's appointed times to meet with us. Would you ignore or arrive late for your set time to meet with the president of the United States? It may not cost you your life, but you would miss a great honor and blessing. How much more of a blessing would you be missing if you stood up God at His set appointment?

God calls the feasts "convocations," which in the Hebrew means "rehearsals" (Lev. 23:2).

> Speak unto the children of Israel, and say unto them,
> The feasts of the Lord, which ye shall proclaim

to be holy *convocations*,—these are my *feasts*.
—LEVITICUS 23:2, HOLY SCRIPTURES,
EMPHASIS ADDED

The King James Version states:

Speak unto the children of Israel, and say unto them, Concerning the feasts of the LORD, which ye shall proclaim to be holy *convocations*, even these are my *feasts*.

—EMPHASIS ADDED

God says we should observe these rehearsals at His appointed times *forever* (Lev. 16:29; 23:14, 21, 31, 41). Since the festivals were such clear shadows of Yeshua's First Coming, they must hold significant keys to His return. How would you like to attend a dress rehearsal of the return of Messiah?

We should observe the feasts (fulfill them) as great celebrations. It is as if God is throwing a party and inviting us to attend. We will observe these festivals in the Millennium (Isa. 66:23; Zech. 14:16). So much revelation about Yeshua is ready to be released as we worship God at these appointed times.

PASSOVER

Looking at the Passover dinner gives us insight about the last days. The first New Covenant Passover was actually an "engagement dinner." It was not just to remember the Exodus from Egypt, but it was a promise of a future exodus from earth.

In ancient Judaism, an engagement was as binding as a marriage. After the engagement, the bridegroom went to prepare a room in his father's house for his bride.

At the Last Supper, Yeshua drank the third cup of wine—"the cup of redemption," which He called the "new covenant in my blood" (Luke 22:20).[1] In the context of the marriage customs of ancient Israel, He was also making a kind of betrothal statement. Earlier, He had told His disciples:

> I go to prepare a place for you. And if I go and prepare a place for you, I will come again and receive you to Myself; that where I am, there you may be also.
> —JOHN 14:2–3

The custom in those days was for a bridegroom to pay a dowry, either in goods or services, to the father of his bride as compensation for the loss of her presence in their household. In drinking the cup of redemption, Yeshua was saying to His bride, the church, "I will redeem you—I will pay the price for you." Yeshua's blood on the cross was the highest price ever paid for a bride. It released the Holy Spirit to assemble this new bride made up of Jews and Gentiles who become "One New Man" in Yeshua.

The fourth cup of wine we drink at the Passover meal is called "the cup of praise." Yeshua did not drink this cup on earth. After the third cup, He said:

> But I say to you, I will not drink of this fruit of the vine from now on until that day when I drink

it new with you in My Father's kingdom.
—MATTHEW 26:29

That day will come when the church, the bride—
the One New Man—is caught up in the air to be
with Yeshua (1 Thess. 4:16–17). We will share with
Him in the marriage supper of the Lamb—a heavenly
Passover meal (Rev. 19:7–9).

BLESSING, NOT BONDAGE

As a traditional Jew, I used to follow the festivals the
same way each year. Eventually, I got bored with traditions learned by rote. When I became a Messianic
Jew, I found there were hidden meanings about the
Messiah in the festivals. I saw purpose in the celebrations. But observing the same events in exactly the
same way—year after year—became boring again. For
me, it became more of a form of entertainment, or
tradition, rather than a spiritual encounter with God.

So what is the answer? We should not necessarily
follow the Rabbinic interpretations and traditions or
even our new Messianic understandings exactly the
same way every time. Instead of being traditional about
how we observe the festivals, we should study each festival in the Scriptures. Then pray, "Holy Spirit, how
can we glorify Yeshua in a special way at this appointed
time?" (For an in-depth look at how your church can
celebrate the biblical festivals in a unique way every
year, see Appendix B.)

Yeshua performed more miracles on the Sabbath
than on any other day. I have found that God increases

the anointing for miracles and evangelism during the festivals. When you celebrate these feasts, you know that God is pleased.

I believe that there are supernatural blessings connected with observing the biblical festivals in liberty. For instance, God specifically states that for those who observe the Sabbath:

> I will give you great honor and give you your full share of the inheritance I promised to Jacob, your ancestor. I, the LORD, have spoken!
> —ISAIAH 58:14, NLT

In the Holy Scriptures (the Jewish approved Scriptures), it says:

> I will cause thee to tread upon the high places of the earth, and I will cause thee to enjoy the inheritance of Jacob thy father; for the mouth of the Lord hath spoken it.

Churches are beginning to use the seven biblical festivals as corporate worship events: Passover, Unleavened Bread, Firstfruits, Pentecost, Trumpets, Day of Atonement, and Tabernacles.

We are told to teach the festivals to our children (Exod. 12:26–27). I believe God would be honored if we set the Sabbath apart for family time. Because of His supernatural promises, God will use this time to restore families. This is a great way for Yeshua to fulfill (or as I say, "fill full of Himself") the fourth commandment.

UNHOLY MERGER

Prophets such as Jeremiah and Hosea forbade the Jewish people to merge paganism with belief in God. (See Jeremiah 7:30–31 and Hosea 3:1.) Jeremiah 2:13 says the people have committed two evils: they have forsaken God's vessel and made their own defective vessels.

> For my people have committed two evils; they have forsaken me the fountain of living waters, and hewed them out cisterns, broken cisterns, that can hold no water.
>
> —KJV

> For two evils have my people committed: me have they forsaken, the source of living waters, to hew out for themselves cisterns, broken cisterns, that cannot hold water.
>
> —HOLY SCRIPTURES

In the early church, Jewish believers in the Messiah were forced by Gentile Christians to give up worship on the Sabbath and other biblical festivals under threat of excommunication or death. As we saw in the previous chapter, these godly shadows and prophetic pictures of the Messiah's First Coming, return, and millennial reign were replaced with pagan traditions.

What are we to do today? Are we to give up Sunday worship? Not necessarily. The key is not that we should abandon Sunday as a day of worship, but that we should repent of the anti-Semitic attitudes of the early church leaders who established Sunday worship.

Does the Bible tell us to worship on Sunday? No. The Bible mentions some gathered on the first day of the week. One reason for this was because tithes, alms giving, and all business could not be conducted on the Sabbath. Nowhere in Scripture are we *commanded* to worship on Sunday.

Many refer to Sunday as "the Lord's day," giving it special significance as a holy day. What is the Lord's day? Psalm 118:24 says, *"This* is the day which the LORD has made; we will rejoice and be glad in it" (emphasis added). Today most Christians worship the Lord on Sunday. But God has selected *every* day to be the day the Lord has made or the "Lord's day." Since Sunday is usually a day we do not have to work, it is a convenient time for corporate worship. However, that doesn't make it the Sabbath.

CELEBRATING IN JOY AND FREEDOM

Hosea 3:4–5 says:

> For the children of Israel shall abide many days without king or prince, without sacrifice or sacred pillar, without ephod or teraphim. Afterward the children of Israel shall return and seek the LORD their God and David their king.

In other words, in the latter days there will be a revival among the Jewish people. This is the set time to favor Zion (Israel). (See Psalm 102:13.)

True repentance, or change in behavior, by the church will release this Jewish revival. What would demonstrate true repentance on behalf of the Christians for the anti-Semitism of the church and forcing the Jewish believers to reject their biblical festivals? Reconciliation meetings have been a good start, but we need to go deeper. Not much has changed. Israel is not saved. What about a step of repentance by restoring the Jewish roots of the faith?

Some congregations will worship only on the Sabbath, which is also known as the *Shabbat*. The biblical Shabbat begins on Friday evening at sundown. Other congregations will worship on Shabbat and Sunday. Instead of a Sunday morning service and a Sunday evening service, how about a Friday evening and a Sunday morning service? Others will take Saturday as a true day of rest, a family day. At this time, this is how I personally observe Shabbat. The seven feasts of the Lord are for Him. He says, "These are My feasts" (Lev. 23:2). But the Sabbath was made for man to rest. "The Sabbath was made for man, and not man for the Sabbath" (Mark 2:27). I am not suggesting a rigid tradition. Pray about it, and do what is pleasing to God. Do not make the Shabbat a legalistic formula. At the same time, do not act as if Sunday worship is a legalistic formula. Never lose sight of the objective. The objective is not Jewish roots, but the Jewish Messiah, who is our Sabbath.

Let me warn you by saying that this is not another segmented ministry of the church such as a singles group or just another meeting like Wednesday night prayer. If that is how you view the Sabbath, then you have missed the Spirit of God. The idea behind a Shabbat service is for the congregation to totally identify with its biblical roots and with the Jewish people and the Jewish Messiah. If the majority attend on Sunday and just a few on Shabbat, you will end up with two congregations. God is after One New Man, not a few segregated events.

Some will take the revelation of Jewish roots and create a legalistic system based on a works mentality. Eventually, these Judaizers will evolve into a denomination and fossilize. A religious spirit will settle on them. Their identity will be in their Jewish culture rather than in the Jewish Messiah. They will cause much disunity in the body. Many in the church will fight this "religious" Jewish roots movement because of the legalists.

Others in the Jewish roots movement will completely divorce themselves from the "Gentile" church and embrace elements of Rabbinic Judaism. Sadly, the anti-Christ spirit of traditional rabbis who deny the deity of Yeshua will infect some. The supernatural allure of man-made tradition attracts these religious spirits. Their ultimate assignment is to make the believer convert to traditional Rabbinic Judaism and renounce Yeshua.

Those same religious spirits can attach themselves to extra-biblical traditions within Christianity. These spirits try to convince the believer that the church has replaced the Jew and Israel. (See chapter three, "Who Is Israel?") This anti-Semitic stance opens the door to other heresies.

The devil tries to get us in a religious ditch on one side of the road or the other—either "Christian" anti-Semitism or Judaism without Yeshua. But a new move of God's Spirit will blow on the church, and a new freedom in biblical festivals will come forth.

CHAPTER 8

The Law of Evangelism

One rainy day in Rockville, Maryland, I decided to visit the Judaic library at the Jewish Community Center. A book on the Jews of China caught my eye. It showed pictures of Chinese Jews from Kaifeng, whose ancestors had come to China many generations earlier. They came as silk merchants and lived in cities that made up the "Silk Route." I also noted the reference to Isaiah 49:12, "Surely these shall come from afar; look! Those from the north and the west, and these from the land of Sinim." The author said the word *Sinim* is Hebrew for "China." *Imagine*, I thought, *God predicted there would be Jews in China*. I had never even heard of a Chinese Jew. Further, God said they would return to Israel in the last days.

In 1995 Bob Weiner, a visiting speaker, told the local church I attended that revival had started in China. Pastor Bill Ligon asked if I wanted to team up with him to take a tour group there. I immediately said, "Yes, if we can go to Kaifeng." My motivation in going to Kaifeng was the Law of Evangelism. I knew if we reached out to the Jew, God would bless our efforts to reach all people.

In Kaifeng I met a Chinese Jew who took me to his family cemetery. He proudly showed me twelve generations of his Jewish ancestors. Another Chinese Jew told me, "I am a Jew. I told my son he is a Jew, and he must live in Israel!" This man knew nothing about Judaism or Christianity. How could he know that thousands of years earlier God had recorded in the Bible that Jews from China would return to Israel? Since that time he and his entire family have immigrated to Israel.

As part of the tour, we brought singers and dancers to Kaifeng to conduct a Feast of Tabernacles celebration. This event was televised throughout the entire city. When we went to the Jew first, God opened up a door to reach the whole area.

DON'T COMPROMISE

A best-selling Christian author has written a book saying that it is unbiblical to "go to the Jew first" with the gospel. He argues that Jewish people have suffered so much they should not be targeted for evangelism by overzealous Christians. A well-meaning Christian who reads this will feel there is no need to evangelize the Jew. Many believers who say they love the Jewish people and Israel share this anti-Semitic thinking. I'm sure they genuinely love the Jew and Israel, but they need to realize that the most anti-Semitic act is *not* to share the gospel. They must be careful not to value their relationship with the Jewish community more highly than their obedience to God's Word.

It is true that after all these centuries of persecution by so-called "Christians," we must love the Jew. Only acts of "supernatural love" will melt the centuries of misunderstandings. But don't fall into the trap of a love without Yeshua.

May the words of Ezekiel 3:17–18 and Acts 4:12 ring in our ears:

> Son of man, I have made you a watchman for the house of Israel....When I say to the wicked, "You shall surely die," and you give him no warning...his blood I will require at your hand.

> Nor is there salvation in any other, for there is no other name under heaven given among men by which we must be saved.

FOLLOW THE PATTERN

The Law of Evangelism is found in Romans 1:16:

> For I am not ashamed of the gospel of [Messiah], for it is the power of God to salvation for everyone who believes, for *the Jew first* and also for the Greek.
> —EMPHASIS ADDED

This was God's *historical* order to reach the world, but it is also God's *spiritual* order.

This pattern is found throughout Scripture. When Yeshua went to the Jew first, it opened up a supernatural door of evangelism for all people. Yeshua commanded His disciples, "Go rather to the lost sheep of the house of Israel" (Matt. 10:6). The Messiah realized that by planting a seed to the "Jew first," it would open the door to evangelize the world. Since the Jewish people have been spread to the four corners of the earth (Isa. 11:12), when you go to the Jews, you reach virtually everyone else, too.

The principle that causes the Law of Evangelism to operate is found in Genesis 12:3. God promises to bless those who bless the Jewish people. As we sow seed into the Jewish people by sharing with them the good news, we will, in turn, reap an abundant harvest among the Gentiles.

John Owen, one of the greatest Puritan theologians, knew this amazing truth of going to the Jew first. He said, "There is not any promise anywhere of raising up a kingdom unto the Lord Jesus Christ in this world but it is either expressed, or clearly intimated, that the beginning of it must be with the Jews."[1]

God says He will pour out His Spirit on all flesh in the last days. As a result, Jewish sons and daughters will prophesy (Joel 2:28). The Jewish people will experience a major revival. The prophet Joel says this will happen at the time the nations try to divide up the land of Israel (Joel 3:2). And it will be the catalyst for the greatest revival in history. Zechariah says:

Thus says the LORD of hosts: "In those days ten men from every language of the nations shall grasp the sleeve [fringes of the prayer shawl] of a Jewish man, saying, 'Let us go with you, for we have heard that God is with you.'"
—ZECHARIAH 8:23

God will cause His former rain (Spirit of God on the Jewish people) and His latter rain (Spirit of God on Christians) to come down at *once* (Joel 2:23). Rain brings life for the harvest. This specific miracle has never happened in history. The supernatural downpour of the two rains simultaneously will bring forth a harvest that will result in multitudes being saved!

YOU AND YOUR HOUSE

When I tell believers they need to reach the Jewish people with the gospel, some are exasperated. "But Sid," they protest, "I have tried to share Yeshua with Jewish people. They are just not interested."

This is God's appointed time to reach Israel. But it can't be done by man's methods. I'm an expert on how it *can't* be done. I have tried just about everything. Although most of these methods have worked to some degree, the revival prophesied in Joel 2:28 has not fully manifested. If it is God's time to reach Jewish people with the gospel and to form the One New Man Glorious Congregation, then how will it take place? God has given me a prophetic example through my father. When I accepted the Lord, he was shocked, outraged, and embarrassed. My dad was born in Poland into a traditional Jewish family. To say the least, he was not raised to love Christianity. He told me that when he was a young boy, his father would spit at a church as they walked past. Whenever I talked about Yeshua, the conversation ended in shouting, anger, and much hurt. My public, vocal witness for Yeshua brought him shame.

My mother was another story. She was also Jewish, but she was born in America. Although she attended the traditional synagogue to please my father, she was not as fervent. When I accepted the Lord, she wasn't happy, but she never let it interfere with her love for me. She was grateful that my experience with God had restored my marriage and made me a far more responsible person.

While my mom tolerated my beliefs, she was not quick to follow them. When I shared prophecies that proved Yeshua was the Jewish Messiah, it didn't faze her. When I prayed for her and others and they were healed, it interested her but didn't change her. Finally, as she observed the peace and fulfillment I had over many years, the Lord broke through and she received Him as the Jewish Messiah.

Immediately after I had my experience with Yeshua, I began to share my testimony. Wherever I spoke I asked people to pray for my father's salvation. My mother was not so hopeful. She would sigh and tell me, "Your father will never believe in Jesus!"

I replied without the slightest doubt, "I *know* he will become a believer." From that point on I began to say often, "I *know* my father will become a believer." I said it so many times that I began to believe it.

My mother didn't want me to be disappointed. She was sure it was impossible for a Jewish person like my father to believe. But Yeshua says in Mark 9:23, "If you can believe, *all* things are possible" (emphasis added). And I had long since moved from hope to faith.

After Mom died, my father asked me to go to the synagogue daily for a year and say a memorial prayer (*Kaddish*) for her. I knew it would not do her any good, because she was already in heaven. But, for my father's sake, I went and said a prayer. Many people at the synagogue who did not like that I was an outspoken believer still told my father I was a good son for going every day to the synagogue. After that year, my dad had many close calls with death. I remember telling people: "Dad can't die. He hasn't received Yeshua yet."

But then I got the call from my sister, Shirley. My father was dying. Shirley and her husband, Marc, had been believers in the Messiah almost as long as I had. "It looks bad," Shirley told me. "You'd better come." Without hesitation, I booked a flight.

Something unusual had happened to me a week earlier. A tangible, wonderful peace from God had come all over my body. This had happened before, but it was different this time. It stayed with me twenty-four hours a day, and it was getting stronger. I didn't know the reason for it, but I was grateful.

When I arrived, I met my sister at the hospital, and we went straight to the intensive care unit. My dad was eighty-three and had prostate cancer. Since the cancer had invaded his bones, we knew he could die at any moment. His voice was so weak he could barely speak above a whisper. I asked, "Dad, don't you want to be in the same place as Mom? She used to say, 'Heaven must be such a wonderful place.' Do you want to make Yeshua your Messiah and Lord?"

He replied, "Yes," and we prayed.

Then my sister said, "Sid, I didn't hear him."

I responded, "Shirley, that was *good* for Dad. *I* heard him."

She put her hands on her hips and said, "I'm not sure. Dad, do you want to make Yeshua your Messiah and Lord?"

My father got his old spunk back and belted out, "Yes!"

With that, Shirley began to jump up and down and scream very loudly, "Thank You, Yeshua! Thank You!" My sister was a conservative schoolteacher, so this outburst was totally out of character for her. Besides, in the intensive care unit everyone is *supposed* to remain very quiet. I tried to calm her down—to no avail. She said, "I promised the Lord I would jump for joy when Dad was saved!"

My father went to heaven the next day.

THE ANOINTING DESTROYS THE YOKE

Many have witnessed to Jewish people without any visible signs of success. As a result, they have stopped witnessing. But now we are in a new season. This is the set time to favor Zion. God must restore the Jewish branches to the olive tree. We cannot have the "glorious church" until the middle wall of separation comes down between Jew and Gentile to birth the One New Man. God is once again having mercy on Israel.

How was my father saved? Remember the anointing that came upon me a week before he died? "And the yoke will be destroyed because of the anointing…" (Isa. 10:27). The anointing of the Holy Spirit destroys the demonic yokes of unbelief. Get ready for the anointing for Jewish evangelism that is being poured out. All things are possible to those who believe. If a Jew like my father can be saved, so can the Jewish person whom God will have cross your path! It is "not by might nor by power, but by My Spirit, says the Lord of hosts" (Zech. 4:6).

A Lamb for a House

I am blessed because my entire family knows Yeshua. This is God's norm. In the Book of Exodus, God says the lamb sacrificed at Passover is for the *entire* household (Exod. 12:3). Noah's entire household was saved from the Flood. The scarlet cord, which represents the blood, protected Rahab's entire family from being killed (Josh. 2:18). Joshua knew the heart of God for families to be saved when he said, "But as for me and *my house*, we will serve the LORD" (Josh. 24:15, emphasis added). When Cornelius, a Gentile, came to accept Yeshua as Savior, it resulted in his whole family being saved as well (Acts 10:24, 44). In Acts 16:31, Paul said to the Philippian jailer, "Believe on the Lord [Yeshua the Messiah], and you will be saved, *you and your household.*"

The Jewish law for family evangelism applies not just to one member of a household but the entire *mishpochah* (family). You *and* your house will be saved! A Lamb for a house!

PART 3
THE LAST LAP

For He Himself is our peace, who has made both one, and has broken down the middle wall of separation...to create in Himself *one new man* from two, thus making peace, and *that He might reconcile them both to God in one body through the cross.*
—EPHESIANS 2:14–16,
EMPHASIS ADDED

CHAPTER 9

Getting Back to Basics

My childhood memories of Passover include the empty place setting at the table for Elijah. Every year we expected the prophet to announce the coming of the Messiah. I would even go to the door and open it just in case Elijah was waiting outside. And every year I would be disappointed.

This practice comes from Malachi 4:5–6:

> Behold, I will send you Elijah the prophet
> Before the coming of the great and dreadful day
>   of the LORD.
> And he will turn
> The hearts of the fathers to the children,
> And the hearts of the children to their fathers,
> Lest I come and strike the earth with a curse.

As I grew up, I realized many traditional Jews did not believe Elijah would ever come—it was just a fable. After I became a Messianic Jew, I learned that Elijah had already come. Yeshua (Jesus) made it clear that "Elijah" in Malachi's prophecy was referring to John the Baptist (Matt. 17:10–13). Luke 1:17 says that John would walk "in the spirit and power of Elijah." In other words, the same spirit that was on Elijah would be on John.

But what about the rest of the prophecy? Paul tells us the "fathers" of the faith are Jewish. (See Romans 9:4–5.) The "children" represent Christians because they have received a spiritual heritage from the Jewish "fathers"—Abraham, Isaac, and Jacob. So Malachi is warning us that if there is not a union of Jews and Christians in the last days, we will receive a curse instead of a blessing.

Remember, the favor of God (Gen. 12:3) followed the Jewish tabernacle. Wherever the tabernacle went, it brought blessing when we were obedient to God. When the Jewish people are restored to the olive tree, it will bring the blessing of God.

This is exactly what Paul saw in Romans 11:12, 15: "Now if their [the Jewish people's] fall is riches for the world, and their failure riches for the Gentiles, how much more their fullness!…For if their being cast away is the reconciling of the world, what will their acceptance be but life from the dead?"

Get ready for the new outpouring of God's Spirit on the dry, dead bones of Israel. It will bring blessings and resurrection life back to the church. It will release the greatest revival in history.

The devil will not take this lying down. Watch out for the greatest deception in church history. Replacement Theology will be rampant. Another of the devil's strategies to delay this next move of God will be to make the Jewish roots movement legalistic.

Religious spirits will cause some Christians to believe that if they don't say God's name in Hebrew or if they don't worship on Saturday, it will cost them their salvation. They will try to make those who celebrate traditional Christian holidays feel like second-class citizens.

Don't get me wrong. I believe there are supernatural blessings in New Covenant expressions of celebrating the feasts. I love to refer to Jesus by His Hebrew name, Yeshua. I love to have my Shabbat (Sabbath) on Saturday—the biblical day God selected. I know that centuries ago many church traditions were merged with pagan practices for political and anti-Jewish reasons. I know how after this happened the church moved from intimacy and power to dead religion.

But *please* do not commit the same error by legislating something God Himself is restoring in New Testament freedom. Let us provoke others to jealousy by the outpouring of God's Spirit and love and power when we worship God on biblical feasts.

On the other hand, the same religious spirits are at work in the Gentile church. Some Christians make you feel as if Sunday worship is required for salvation. Others act as if you are betraying the faith if you object to the paganism mixed into Easter and Christmas or if you use Hebrew names.

For revival to spread we will need a lot more loving and a lot less judging.

We are approaching the time of Jacob's trouble. "Alas! For that day is great, so that none is like it; and it is the time of Jacob's trouble, but he shall be saved out of it" (Jer. 30:7). This will be the worst time of persecution in history, first for the Jew and then for the Christian. When persecution hits, which day we worship or how we worship will not be as important as *whom* we worship.

The supernatural blessings that will be released when the church evangelizes the Jew are needed now! The salvation of Israel is necessary for the emergence of the Elijah generation, and the Elijah generation will prepare the way of the Lord. The Gentile Christian needs the piece of the puzzle the Jewish believer has, and the Jewish believer needs the part of the puzzle the Gentile Christian has—and we all need Yeshua.

These are the days of Elijah!

THE ONE NEW MAN GLORIOUS CONGREGATION

What would the church be like today if we started from scratch and just followed the Scriptures? What would happen if we squeezed all tradition from Judaism and Christianity, and Jews and Christians came together as one? Let me introduce you to the Glorious Congregation—the emergence of the One New Man—Yeshua!

Although Malachi is the last book in the Christian Old Testament, 2 Chronicles is the last book in the Jewish

Old Testament, or as we Jewish people would say, the Tenach. The Tenach presents the Books of Scripture in a different order. I believe that the last words in the Tenach must have great prophetic significance.

The Tenach closes with this prophetic word:

> Thus hath said Cyrus the king of Persia, All the kingdoms of the earth hath the Lord the God of heaven given me; and he *hath charged me to build him a house in Jerusalem, which is in Judah.* Whoever there is among you of all his people, may the Lord his God be with him, and let him go up.
> —2 CHRONICLES 36:23, HOLY SCRIPTURES,
> EMPHASIS ADDED

The spiritual fulfillment of these words will reach its highest expression in the One New Man Congregation of Jew and Gentile believers.

God says we are to build Him a house [temple]. (See Ephesians 2:14–15, 22.) His objective is to "gather together in *one* all things in [Messiah]" (Eph. 1:10, emphasis added). When the wall between Jew and Gentile is removed, the spiritual temple, God's dwelling place, will be restored, and this One New Man will release resurrection power to the church that Paul calls "life from the dead" (Rom. 11:15)!

How can the devil stop the explosion of God's power? *How can he stop the building of the temple?* If the foundation is destroyed, the temple cannot be built. What is the strategy? Stop Jews from seeing the Messiah and becoming "one" with Gentile believers.

THE TABERNACLE OF DAVID

The tabernacle of David in 1 Chronicles 16 is a prophetic symbol of the "One New Man." In the tabernacle of David, there was no separation between the people and God. There was no "holy of holies." Everyone experienced God's presence. David instituted daily praise before the Lord (1 Chron. 16:37), and the Levites worshiped God with the songs of David.

The tabernacle of David prophesied by Amos is also a type of the One New Man Glorious Congregation.

> "On that day I will raise up
> The tabernacle ['house' or 'family'] of David
>   [the Jewish people], which has fallen down,
> And repair its damages;
> I will raise up its ruins,
> And rebuild it as in the days of old;
> That they may possess the remnant of Edom
>   [Septuagint reads 'mankind'],
> And all the Gentiles who are called by My
>   name,"
> Says the LORD who does this thing.
> —AMOS 9:11–12

God promised that once revival hit the tabernacle (family) of David (the Jewish people), it would cause a revival among the Gentiles (Amos 9:12). In fact, this was the proof text to convince the apostles at the Jerusalem Council meeting to evangelize the Gentiles (Acts 15:16–17).

Amos 9:13 says the blessings of revival will be so

great that the reaper will not be able to gather all the harvest before the next planting season begins. The plowman will overtake the reaper.

If Gentiles were the missing part of the church at the time of the Jerusalem Council meeting of Acts 15, who is missing now? After Yeshua died, the veil of the temple was torn in two (Matt. 27:51). Now nothing should separate us from intimacy with God. Yet, the middle wall of division (veil) between Jews and Gentiles hinders the church from achieving its full destiny in God (Eph. 2:14).

If we want to see and experience God's glory here on earth, then we need to knock down the wall of division that separates us.

Do You Want to See His Face?

Moses saw God's glory, but he could not look at His face.

> And [Moses] said, "Please, show me Your glory."...But He said, "You cannot see My face; for no man shall see Me, and live."
> —Exodus 33:18, 20

After being in God's presence, the glory on Moses' face was so intense that he had to wear a veil or the brightness would blind the people who looked at him as though they were gazing directly into the sun.

The glory of the Old Covenant tabernacle was so thick that, at times, Moses could not even enter (Exod. 40:35). When the cloud of God's glory filled Solomon's temple, the priests could not stand (2 Chron. 5:14). Under the New Covenant, our bodies are temples of the Holy Spirit (1 Cor. 6:19). If the Old Covenant glory was so strong, how much greater glory will fill our New Covenant temples when Jew and Gentile become One New Man in Yeshua.

When will this happen? Psalm 102:13–16 states:

> You will arise and have mercy on Zion;
> For the time to favor her,
> Yes, the set time, has come.
> For Your servants take pleasure in her stones,
> And show favor to her dust.
> So the nations shall fear the name of the LORD,
> And all the kings of the earth Your glory.
> For the LORD shall build up Zion;
> He shall appear in His glory.

When the servants, the Jewish people, take pleasure in (or return to) Israel, the Lord will build up Zion (Jerusalem). When the Lord builds up Zion, He will appear in His glory. This prophecy was written for "the generation to come" (v. 18). The Hebrew could be translated, "for the *last* generation."

This last generation will be uniquely created to restore Davidic praise and worship in order to prepare a tabernacle for the King. Romans 9:4 says the Jewish people will bring the "service" or "worship." This will create a new dimension of worship.

As magnificent Levitical worship is restored, it will bring an outpouring of the same glory that was in Solomon's temple. The Old Covenant glory is the former rain. When the former rain teams up with the latter rain, or the New Covenant glory, we will experience a move of God like the world has never seen.

MIRACLES IN KIEV

The closest to this outpouring I have experienced to date is in the world's largest Messianic Jewish congregation in Kiev, Ukraine. The leader, Rabbi Boris, is always in the Spirit where he receives direction from God. When he implements these instructions, the congregation flourishes. What is his secret? Boris has surrendered to the Holy Spirit.

Over one thousand Jews and Gentiles gather to worship every Saturday in Boris's congregation. There are normally at least one hundred instant healings in *every* service. God instructed Boris to use old-style Chassidic (Orthodox Jewish) worship. The music and dancing are so infectious that almost everyone joins in.

Music usually precedes the move of God. The music that will usher in the One New Man will be a brand-new song. It will be the same music described in Revelation 15:3—the song of Moses (Jew) and the song of the Lamb (Christian) becoming one.

It will be a love song from the bride to her heavenly Bridegroom, from the church to Yeshua. Eye has not seen and ear has not heard what will happen as the bride and Bridegroom increase in intimacy.

Have you ever been to a Jewish wedding? As great as they are on earth, I want to invite you to the best one ever. You have a golden invitation to the marriage supper of the Lamb.

FULL CIRCLE

Everything is about to come full circle. The first to get the good news were the Jewish people, but they will also be the last to get the gospel. Yeshua said, "So the last will be first, and the first last" (Matt. 20:16). God is about ready to move the Jew and Israel to center stage once again.

It is as though we are watching a video of church history in reverse. The closer we get to the return of the Messiah, the more we will look like the first church, and the focus of the world will be on the Jew and Israel.

The restoration of the Jewish roots of the church is happening before our eyes. The church will become more Hebraic in culture. Jewish believers will move into leadership in the church, just as it was at first. There also will be a restoration of the temple, both physical and spiritual. And, of course, the Jews are already returning to Israel.

Although I have presented many of the ingredients of the One New Man Congregation, it will include much more. The one thing for sure is that the next, greatest, and last move of God's Spirit will be different from anything any of us has ever seen.

CHAPTER 10

The Anchor

D id you ever play the game of "telephone" as a child? One person whispers a phrase into another person's ear. By the time the message passes through several people, it is completely distorted. This is what has happened in the church. Down through the ages, customs and traditions have distorted the truth of God's Word. We have wandered from the old paths. We need a more far-reaching reformation than the one started by Martin Luther. We need to return to the God of our fathers. All the way back.

Many years ago I heard about a unique tradition at an Orthodox synagogue in Washington DC. Whenever someone went to the platform to read from the Torah, he would bend his knees and lower his head about a foot, then stand back up before he got to the Torah scroll. Many years later a curious member asked, "Rabbi, why do we dip so low before reading the Torah?" The rabbi explained that the synagogue had previously been located in the basement of another building. Just in front of the Torah was a low water pipe. The only way to get to the Scriptures without hitting your head was to dip low.

As a Jew, I have experienced enough tradition to last a lifetime. But Christianity is loaded with tradition as well. Tradition is a human problem. We all have patterns with which we feel most comfortable. A pastor feels he has to accommodate all these comfort zones. If he is unsuccessful, he often burns out or quits. If he succeeds, the spiritual development of the church is hindered.

Religious groups that have been around the longest have the most tradition. For instance, we Jewish people have more tradition than the Catholics. The Catholics have more tradition than the Protestants. Pentecostals have more tradition than the Charismatics who, in turn, have more tradition than the Word of Faith movement. You get the idea. After going to a specific church for many years, tradition sets in. You find yourself uncomfortable in other expressions in the body of Messiah.

What would happen if the church that always wears choir robes suddenly cast them aside? What if the drums, bass, and guitar were to get very loud in a traditional service? What would happen if the pastor appeared on a Sunday morning with no tie or suit? On the other hand, for those of you who attend a church where the members dress casually, how would you react if your pastor showed up in a suit and tie?

What if there was no "special" music before the pastor spoke? Or what if the pastor suddenly started shaking under the power of God and others began wailing and travailing in the Spirit? What if a mighty wind with flames of fire came into your church building and people started speaking in tongues and acting like they were drunk? (See Acts 2:1–15.)

What would happen if our congregations were more "God sensitive" than "seeker sensitive"? What is more important: God showing up or your traditional order of service?

If the pastor yields to the Spirit, he will immediately start a membership drive—he will drive the members who are preventing revival right out of his church. Some members will say, "I have been a believer for thirty years, and God has never worked that way." Others will be uncomfortable because the pastor is preaching the lordship of Yeshua—not a watered-down version of a cheap life insurance policy. It will not be two hymns, a hum, and out by noon. The entertainment mode will be gone forever, may it rest in peace.

On occasion the pastor might be so caught up into worship that a service could end without him bringing something from the Word. Members might be forced to experience the "Living Word." Children and teenagers will not be shipped out to watch videos. They will all be at the front of the church weeping for the lost.

HOME SWEET HOME (CHURCH)

The early church met in houses. Acts 2:46 says that they were "breaking bread from house to house." Everyone participated at these house meetings.

> Whenever you come together, *each of you* has a psalm, has a teaching, has a tongue, has a revelation, has an interpretation.
> —1 CORINTHIANS 14:26, EMPHASIS ADDED

How is this possible in a large meeting? It's not.

An ideal place to do this is in home meetings like the early church.

The emphasis in these meetings will not be on the "one man show," but on the "One New Man body." The people will really get to know one another. They will become *mishpochah* (Hebrew for "family") by sharing meals and demonstrating God's kingdom on earth. The leader's job will be to offer maturity and surrender control to the lordship of the Holy Spirit. Instead of a worship team leading the music, everyone will participate. As a new believer, I used to attend the Catholic Charismatic prayer meetings. When the Holy Spirit took over worship, it was breathtaking.

Even the sermons in these home meetings may sometimes be very different. At times as God's Spirit is leading the meeting, many will share, and their short words will form a tapestry of God's message for that time and place.

Because people will become *participants* rather than *spectators*, the groups will grow in leadership and gifting.

These smaller meetings will restore the Jewish mind-set as opposed to the Greco-Roman approach. The biblical Jewish way is worshiping and acknowledging God and placing Him first in a total commitment, twenty-four hours a day, seven days a week. Part of the Greco-Roman perspective is worshiping or acknowledging God only at certain times.

Miracles will become common in home groups that are yielded to God's Spirit. Believers will be added continually because they will be attracted to the love and unity within the group. People are love-starved and need to experience God's kingdom demonstrated on earth. Everyone will be a productive, functioning member. Everyone will find their gifts and use them. I firmly believe that the church just before Messiah returns will be home churches.

NEW WINESKINS

Many in the church today feel a godly discontent. We know the old manna doesn't taste good any longer. We are crying out for something more. We hunger for greater intimacy with God. Our old wineskins cannot contain the glory that is coming to the church.

The bridegroom at the wedding in Cana was told by the master of the feast, "You have kept the good wine until now" (John 2:10). The best wine, a type of the Holy Spirit, is about to be poured out. But the old system (institutional Christianity or church) will not contain the glory. We need a new wineskin (Matt. 9:17).

God is preparing to release His champion, His One New Man, for the last lap. But first the wineskins must be changed to contain the outpouring of His Spirit.

Lord, You know I don't have all the answers, but You do. You love Your church. Please restore to us the joy of our salvation. Replace our old wineskins with new wineskins so that when You pour out Your Spirit, we can receive all that You have for us. Give us the courage to scrap the man-made foundations in order to be able to contain the glory of the One New Man anointing. Show us what it means to put on the One New Man (Eph. 4:24).

CHAPTER 11

Truth or Consequences

God's Word commands us to pray for the peace of Jerusalem. *"Pray for the peace of Jerusalem: 'May they prosper who love you'"* (Ps. 122:6). The word *prosper* refers to something more important than money. In Hebrew it means, "heart peace."

Jerusalem means "City of Peace." One day soon Yeshua will rule Jerusalem and the Word of the Lord will be broadcast from that city to the whole world. (See Isaiah 2:1–4.)

When we pray for the peace of Jerusalem, we are praying for the return of Messiah Yeshua. We are praying for Jerusalem to become the true "City of Peace." We are praying for worldwide revival. We are praying for Jewish unbelievers to be saved so the world can believe. We are praying for the completion of the One New Man.

The devil and his crowd are doing everything possible to abort God's plan. Yeshua said He would not return until the Jewish people say, "Blessed is He who comes in the name of the Lord!" (Matt. 23:39). But this does not concern the devil as much as the great harvest that will come when the Jewish branch is grafted back into the olive tree. It will cause the life of God to explode through His One New Man to a dying humanity (Rom. 11:15).

DIVIDING THE SHEEP FROM THE GOATS

The plumbline for the church and the nations is always Israel. Genesis 12:3, where God promises to bless those who bless the Jewish people and curse those who curse them, is still true. How much more so at this set time to favor Zion!

All the earth is the Lord's, and He has assigned Israel to the Jewish people. A summary of His mandate is found in Psalm 105:8–11. God says He gives the land of Israel (Canaan) to the Jewish people "forever," for "everlasting," and "for a thousand generations." Three different ways He says the same thing. It must be important.

A biblical Zionist believes the Jewish people are given the land of Israel forever. Obviously, God was the first Zionist.

God says in Matthew 25:31–46 that nations will be divided as a shepherd separates goats from sheep. A goat has a mind of its own, but a sheep follows the shepherd. Yeshua tells us what the dividing line will be: "Assuredly, I say to you, inasmuch as you did it to one of the least of these My brethren [Greek means "from the womb"—the Jewish people], you did it to Me" (Matt. 25:40). The same single judgment issue is mentioned prophetically in Joel 3:2:

> I will also gather all nations…and *I will enter into judgment* with them there *on account of My people, My heritage Israel,* whom they have scattered among the nations, *they have also divided up My land.*
>
> —EMPHASIS ADDED

WARNING JUDGMENTS

The United States, as a nation, has violated every one of the Ten Commandments. We are hanging by a single thread. One of the main reasons we still enjoy some of God's favor is because we are friends with Israel. However, we are dangerously close to losing that blessing. God always warns before judgment to allow for repentance. He is giving His final warning to America.

> Anyone who harms you [Israel] harms my most precious possession. I [God] will raise my fist to crush them.
>
> — ZECHARIAH 2:8–9, NLT

John McTernan, in his book *God's Final Warning to America*, documents that when America has gone against Israel we have suffered "warning judgments."[1] Former President George Bush initiated his 1991 peace plan for the Middle East right after the Gulf

War. As part of that plan, he tried to pressure Israel to surrender land for peace. God promised this land to the Jewish people forever. Is it just a coincidence that, despite enjoying historically high approval ratings after the Gulf War, Bush lost his bid for reelection?

When the United States pressures Israel to give away her land, warning judgments befall America almost simultaneously! Proverbs 26:2 says, "So a curse without cause shall not alight."

- On October 30, 1991, former President Bush gave a speech to open the "land for peace" conference in Madrid, Spain. The next day, one of the most powerful storms to have ever occurred in the United States smashed into New England. The storm damaged the East Coast from Maine to Florida. Thirty-foot waves pounded President Bush's home in Kennebunkport, Maine, inflicting heavy damage.[2] A book and a movie later came out about this massive storm called *The Perfect Storm.*

- On August 23, 1992, the Madrid Peace Conference was transferred to Washington DC. The very first day of the conference Hurricane Andrew hit southern Florida. At that time, Andrew was the worst natural disaster ever to hit the United States![3]

- In January 1998, President Bill Clinton met with Israeli Prime Minister Benjamin Netanyahu to pressure him to give up land

for peace. Soon after, while Clinton was
waiting for a meeting with Yasser Arafat, the
nation learned of Clinton's indiscretion with
a White House intern.[4]

These are just a few of the many warnings. If these
are just the warnings, imagine what the judgments
will be like. God is serious. Time is running short.
As a nation, we need to remain true to His Word and
remain true to the nation of Israel.

CHAPTER 12

For Such a Time As This

believe the Book of Esther is *the* End-Time book for the church. God is the real hero in this book, although His name is not even mentioned. There are four main characters: Ahasuerus (the Gentile king), Esther (the Jewish queen), Mordecai (who adopted, raised, and nurtured Esther), and Haman (who hated the Jewish people).

Esther is symbolic of the Gentile church, and Mordecai is symbolic of the Messiah. Although Esther became queen, she remained totally obedient to Mordecai.

Jewish people have two names. They have a Hebrew name and a name from their homeland. For instance, my English name is "Sid" and my Hebrew name is "Israel." Esther's Hebrew name was "Hadassah," which means "myrtle" (an aromatic shrub), and her Persian name was "Ishtar" (anglicized to "Esther"). *Ishtar* (or Esther) comes from the name of the pagan fertility goddess *Ishtar*. However, *Ishtar*, when translated into Hebrew means "to hide."

Esther was a beautiful virgin, an orphan who had such supernatural favor that she rose to royalty. In Yeshua, the Gentile church is a beautiful virgin. Though adopted (grafted in), Gentiles have risen to become kings and queens in God's kingdom. The church, like Esther, has hidden her Jewish roots and is dressed in Persian, "Ishtar," clothes.

Esther is a book of split-second timing and instant obedience. This is why her preparation was so necessary for this *kairos* moment. Before going to the king, Esther had to soak in oil of myrrh for six months. The myrrh shrub is bitter on the outside, but sweet on the inside. The soaking allowed her spirit (inside) to dominate her flesh (outside). Then she soaked in perfumes for another six months.

Esther, church, as you spend time soaking in God's presence, you will change. This preparation for your appointment with the King will make the difference between being in the outer court and becoming His bride.

After Esther soaked for a year, she thought she was ready, but God knew better. She had to wait another three years before she went to the king. She had an opportunity to get bitter or better. After all, she was beautiful and gifted, yet seemingly placed on a shelf. Spiritually speaking, she could have been like the five foolish virgins of Matthew 25. Instead, like the five wise virgins, she prepared herself to meet the king by cultivating humility and intimacy with God.

THE HAMAN SPIRIT

Haman, the prime minister of Persia and second in command in the kingdom, erected gallows to hang Mordecai when Mordecai refused to bow down to him. However, just as the tree raised to crucify Yeshua resulted in the deathblow to the devil, the tree raised to hang Mordecai resulted in Haman's death (1 Cor. 2:8).

Haman's ancestors were the Amalekites. God knew the Amalekites would be used to fight the Jewish people throughout history. This is why He said in Exodus 17:16, "The LORD will have war with Amalek from generation to generation."

The Haman spirit is rising up again worldwide. The Amalekite (Haman) spirit even rests under the surface in America. Watch as the Jew is blamed for the next economic collapse in America. Haman bribed the king with ten thousand talents of silver for permission to destroy all the Jews. This Amalekite spirit controls the United Nations as well as the U.S. State Department. What will you do, Esther, when the oil-rich Arab countries say to reject Israel or there will be no gasoline?

THE ESTHER ANOINTING

In the Book of Esther, we see the devil's strategy was to murder *all* the Jewish people. Throughout the Bible and the history of mankind, Satan has always attempted to annihilate Jews from the earth. Satan believed that if he could destroy the Jew, he could prevent the coming of the Messiah. Even after Yeshua came, Satan has tried to destroy the Jew because he understands the significance of the One New Man. Without the Jew, there will be no One New Man.

Queen Esther was the *only* one who could go to the king to save the Jewish people. She could have just enjoyed her life of royalty without taking any risks. Some in the church today continue to soak in the anointing and do nothing.

Esther knew it was life-threatening to reveal her Jewish connection. But it would have been more dangerous to keep quiet. Mordecai warned Esther: "Do not think in your heart that you will escape in the king's palace any more than all the other Jews" (Esther 4:13). Some Gentiles might think anti-Semitism doesn't affect them. But after the devil turns against the Jew, he will come after the Christian.

> For if you remain completely silent at this time, relief and deliverance will arise for the Jews from another place, but you and your father's house will perish. Yet who knows whether you have come to the kingdom for such a time as this?
> —ESTHER 4:14

Although in the natural the destruction of the Jewish people was sealed, Esther tapped into the higher laws of the invisible kingdom. After prayer and fasting, a great miracle took place. Instead of being annihilated, the Jewish people "overpowered those who hated them" (Esther 9:1). As a result of the Jewish people being armed with the "sword," a type of the Word of God (Esther 9:5), revival broke out throughout the land among the Gentiles (Esther 8:17)!

I pray in Yeshua's name that you receive the same anointing that was on Queen Esther. I pray you will have the heart of Ruth and say, "Your people [the Jewish people] shall be my people, and your God, my God" (Ruth 1:16).

God's pattern is the same today. Salvation has come to the Gentile church:

- To provoke the Jew to jealousy

- To form the One New Man

- *To save the world*

Yet who knows whether you have come to the kingdom for such a time as this?
—ESTHER 4:14

APPENDICES

What Is Replacement Theology?

The core belief of Replacement Theology is the teaching that the church has replaced Israel and the Jewish people in God's divine plan. All the promises to the Jew and Israel now belong exclusively to the church. In other words, the church gets all the blessings that really belong to the Jews.

In 1948, many of those who believed in Replacement Theology (RT) had a change of heart when the State of Israel was reestablished. They realized God's promises were literal as well as spiritual. He never went back on His promises to the physical nation of Israel. Paul puts it this way: "For the gifts and the calling of God are irrevocable" (Rom. 11:29). The prophet Jeremiah writes, "If heaven above can be measured, and the foundations of the earth searched out beneath, I will also cast off all the seed of Israel for all they have done, says the LORD" (Jer. 31:37). If you can trust God with His promises to the physical seed of Israel (the Jewish people), you can trust Him with His promises to the spiritual seed of Israel (the church)!

Why can't the church be the "new Israel"?

A fair reading of Romans 9–11 answers this question. For instance, Romans 11:28 is talking about Israel. Some say it now means the "church" and the church has replaced Israel. Let's insert the word "church" instead of Israel and see how it reads: "Concerning the gospel they [the church] are the enemies for your sake, but concerning the election they [the church] are beloved for the sake of the fathers." The church is not God's enemy! The church is not beloved for the promises to the fathers—Abraham, Isaac, and Jacob. The Jewish people are beloved for the sake of the promises to the Jewish fathers. Obviously, the church has not replaced Israel.

Let's turn to a modern-day version found in *The Message*, for a clearer understanding of Romans 11:28–29:

> From your point of view as you hear and embrace the good news of the Message, it looks like the Jews are God's enemies. But looked at from the long-range perspective of God's overall purpose, they remain God's oldest friends. God's gifts and God's call are under full warranty—never canceled, never rescinded.

The simple fact that many Gentiles embraced the gospel message and Yeshua, while many Jews rejected

Yeshua as Messiah, does not make Jews God's enemies! God's purpose was to reach His beloved—the
Jews—first and then the Gentile. The Jewish people
are forever beloved for the sake of God's promises to
the Jewish forefathers.

Could the terms *Jew* or *Israel* in Scripture sometimes refer to the church?

The terms *Jew* or *Jews* are found over 190 times in
the New Testament. They are always used to describe
the Jewish people. They never refer to a Gentile Christian. The 77 references to "Israel" always refer to the
land of Israel or to the Jewish people.

But what about Galatians 3:28, "…there is neither Jew nor Greek"? Doesn't that mean there is no longer a special calling on the Jewish people?

You must keep reading. The verse goes on to say "there
is neither male nor female." Paul is saying in Yeshua we
are all the "new creation," "the body of Messiah." But
as long as this earth exists in the natural realm there will
be males and females, Jews and Gentiles. Although we
become a "new creation" in Messiah, we still keep our
own gender and national identity. This is why James
could address his letter to the twelve tribes (of Israel).
He still saw Jewish believers in Yeshua as Israelites. In
Romans 9:4, Paul even calls Jews who have rejected
the Messiah "Israelites." Paul refers to himself as a Jew
after becoming a believer (Acts 21:39). Although we are
all equal, the Bible has different callings for males and
females as well as Jews and Gentiles.

What is God's special calling on the Gentile?

Paul says, "…to provoke them [Jewish people] to jealousy, salvation has come to the Gentiles" (Rom. 11:11). Gentile Christians owe a debt of gratitude to the first Jewish believers in Yeshua. God's brilliant plan is for Gentile Christians to repay this debt by taking the gospel back to the Jew. This opens a door of blessing for the church as well as the individual Christian. (See Genesis 12:3.)

WHAT IS "TWO-COVENANT THEOLOGY"?

Because the evidence is so overwhelming against Replacement Theology, the devil has developed more subtle, hybrid versions of the teaching.

One is called *"Two-Covenant* Theology." Many people who love the Jew cannot accept that those Jewish people who do not believe in Yeshua will be eternally separated from God. They believe a Jew has a covenant with God that eliminates the necessity of believing in Yeshua. This is not true. The Mosaic Covenant requires an animal sacrifice *in the temple* for forgiveness of sin. (See Leviticus 1:5; 17:11.) Since there is no temple, there can be no bloodshed for the atonement of sins. Hebrews 9:22 says, "Without shedding of blood there is *no remission* [for sin]."

Yeshua died—once and for all—and rose again. He has paid the ultimate price by shedding His own blood. Therefore, He is the only way to salvation (John 14:6).

Since there are no animal sacrifices, won't God accept repentance alone by a good traditional Jew?

No. Acts 4:12 says, about belief in Yeshua, that "there is no other name under heaven given among men by which we must be saved."

In Romans 11:26, Paul says, "All Israel will be saved." So why witness to the Jewish people?

Many Jewish people will die without knowing God *before* their national day of visitation. Only those who are *alive* in Israel will be rescued.

WHAT IS "TWO-HOUSE THEOLOGY"?

An even subtler version of Replacement Theology is called *"Two-House* Theology." This is based on the belief that the ten *northern* tribes of Israel are lost among the nations. Proponents believe that any Gentile Christian who follows the Torah is part of these lost tribes. They even call themselves "Israel" or "Ephraim." Furthermore, they say that the people who identify themselves as Jews today are really from the tribe of Judah (the *southern* tribes).

However, just because a Gentile Christian has a heart to follow the Torah does not make him a physical Jew. Furthermore, the "lost tribes" are not lost. (See chapter one.) *We have identified representatives of all the tribes of Israel.*

Paul called himself a "Jew" and *also* called himself an "Israelite." (See Acts 21:39; Romans 11:1.) Why did he call himself an "Israelite" if Israel was lost among the Gentiles? James also knew they were in existence and not totally assimilated in the nations. He writes to them in James 1:1, "to the *twelve* tribes which are scattered abroad."

The terms *Jew* and *Israel* are used interchangeably throughout the New Covenant. Although the northern kingdom of Israel was destroyed in 749 B.C., representatives of all twelve tribes lived in Israel, and all twelve tribes were called "Israel."

Followers of the Two-House Theology love the Jewish people, but they take the spiritual truth of Jew and Gentile becoming "One New Man" too far. They are trying to become "physical" Israel, as though this will give them a special place in God's kingdom. They are wrong. The special place in the kingdom is being a child of God.

What Scriptures will help the Gentile Christian understand he does not have to become Jewish to be special to God?

Those Christians who feel "second-class" because they are not Jewish should look to the parable of the prodigal son. The father represents Father God. The older son represents the Gentile Christian who has worked in the harvest for the last two thousand years. When the younger son (a type of the Jewish believer) comes back home, the older son is jealous. After all, *he* did all the work. The love of Father God is revealed when He says to the older son, "*All that I have is yours*" (Luke 15:31).

It is essential for the church to have a proper understanding of the One New Man of Ephesians 2:14–16.

The Jewish believer in Jesus needs the Gentile believer, and the Gentile believer needs the Jewish believer. Without the Jew *and* Gentile there would be *no* One New Man. We are all equal but incomplete without each other. Be satisfied with who God made you. He doesn't make mistakes.

Celebrate the Feasts

My friend Dr. John Fischer, a Jewish believer in Yeshua, gives his overview of the biblical and spiritual meaning of all the festivals.[1] After the description of each feast, my friend Rabbi Eric Carlson, leader of a One New Man congregation, explains how his congregation celebrates these feasts. The sections labeled "Overview of..." were written by Dr. Fischer. The sections labeled "How to Celebrate..." were written by Rabbi Carlson.

What brings these celebrations to life is that they are filled with the Spirit of God because His Spirit shows you how He wants you to observe them every year. No more "same-old, same-old." Expect a visitation from God.

OVERVIEW OF PASSOVER WEEK

Pesach

Exodus 12 and the earlier chapters tell the story of Pesach (Passover). Nine plagues had not convinced Pharaoh of Egypt to release the Jewish people. God had one final plague in mind. In order to be protected from this plague, each Jewish family had to kill a lamb and apply its blood to the door of their home. When the angel of destruction passed through Egypt, he "passed over" the homes that had the lamb's blood on the door.

Traditionally, Pesach is observed much as it has been since before Yeshua. The major exceptions include the presence of the lamb bone replacing the eating of the lamb and the addition of the *Afikomen* (broken middle *matzah*, the so-called "dessert").[2]

An incident from the time of the second temple highlights the Messianic significance of Pesach. At that time people traveled great distances to observe the holiday in Jerusalem. They would then go to the temple area to select a lamb for the festival. There the priest would indicate an appropriate lamb by pointing to the animal and saying, "Behold the lamb." On one occasion John the Baptist, the son of a priest, saw Yeshua coming in the distance, pointed, and said, "Look, the Lamb..." But he went on to complete his statement, "...of God, who takes away the sin of the world!" (John 1:29, NIV). He thus indicated that Yeshua's forthcoming sacrificial death was related to the meaning of Pesach. Later, the apostle Paul stated, "For Christ [Yeshua], our Passover lamb, has been sacrificed" (1 Cor. 5:7, NIV).

Yeshua the Messiah acted as God's Passover lamb for us; He died that we might live. Before He died, Yeshua took one of the cups of wine during Pesach and said that it represented His blood, which would shortly be shed on our behalf for the forgiveness of sins. (See Matthew 26:27–28.) This would have reminded His followers of the blood of the Passover lamb that was applied to the doorposts back in Egypt.

Now, as we celebrate Pesach, we remember not only God's actions during the time of the Exodus but also Yeshua's death for us, which secured our atonement. In fact, the term used for the piece of matzot that is "hidden" during the Pesach meal, *Afikomen*—a Greek, not Hebrew, term—literally means "the one who came." It was used in the first couple of centuries as a title of Yeshua the Messiah.[3]

Feast of Unleavened Bread

Leviticus 23:6–8 describes this festival, which is closely connected to Pesach and also uses unleavened bread. Unleavened bread (matzot) may well picture "pure" bread in that it has no yeast-like agents. In this sense it remains "uncontaminated." For this reason, leaven frequently represented evil (1 Cor. 5:6–7). This feast became part of the Passover week observance because of the command to eat matzot for seven days during Pesach (Exod. 12:18).

When Yeshua ate His last Passover meal, He took the matzot, broke it—as we do even today—and said it represented His body, which would be given as a sacrifice for us (Matt. 26:26), hence, the significance of "pure" or unleavened bread.

Ceremony of Firstfruits

According to Leviticus 23:9–14, the ceremony of firstfruits occurs immediately after Pesach. The very first part of the harvest is waved before God, a symbolic way of presenting it to God, "so it will be accepted on your behalf" (v. 11, NIV). Traditional observance associates this ceremony with Passover week. The beginning of the fifty-day period of counting the omer, observed by traditional Jews, reflects this ceremony today.

Three days after His death and right after Pesach, Yeshua rose from the dead (Matt. 28:1f). The apostle Paul wrote that by rising from the dead, Yeshua became "the *firstfruits* of those who have fallen asleep [died]" (1 Cor. 15:20, NIV, emphasis added). Like the firstfruits in Leviticus 23:11, His resurrection was "accepted for us" as He was "raised…for our justification" (Rom. 4:25, NIV). So the ceremony of the firstfruits and its traditional counterpart, the beginning of the counting of the omer, should remind us of Yeshua's resurrection. The Resurrection demonstrated that He was indeed the Messiah and that His sacrifice had in fact secured atonement for us.

As we recall the significance of Passover week, we recognize several truths. The blood of the Passover lamb reminds us of Yeshua's great loss of blood at His crucifixion, and the matzot recalls His body sacrificed on our behalf. These holidays picture His death. The ceremony of firstfruits pictures His resurrection. Thus, the Messianic significance of Passover week relates to the atonement made for us by Yeshua the Messiah, effected by His death and resurrection.

HOW TO CELEBRATE PESACH (PASSOVER)

The first thing we do as a One New Man congregation when feast days approach is pray, fast, and seek God's guidance through the Holy Spirit on how to celebrate. We could perform the traditional liturgical celebration, but we prefer serving God and His will today. He desires us to have celebrations where "life" abounds, and He is present. It is nothing short of supernatural how strongly the Holy Spirit works if we step aside and let Him move freely. Feast-day celebrations bring revival (2 Chron. 30). The hardest aspect to overcome in the flesh (especially for pastors) is to step aside and let God and the Holy Spirit work. We must humbly submit ourselves to God in truth and love so that the Holy Spirit can move freely.

When we pray and submit ourselves to God and ask what to do, He always answers, *always!* Here are a few Passover examples of what the Holy Spirit has led us to do in previous years. I am not saying you should celebrate the same way we do, and I am not saying you should not. I am merely giving examples of how the Spirit leads us as a congregation and giving you something to pray and think about.

One year we wrote a short play telling the Passover story. At the conclusion of the play, we circulated

Communion elements—matzot and grape juice—and held Communion. That year six Orthodox Jews who saw the Jewish Messiah in this play partook of Communion with us and accepted Yeshua. Another year we used a rough outline of a traditional Seder (order of service). We placed a Seder plate on every table with the various items, matzot, and grape juice. Using the items on the Seder plate as symbols, we taught how sin is bondage and how we have been delivered from the bondage of sin by the Perfect Lamb, Yeshua. We then took the matzot and juice, had Communion, and worshiped in music and dance for several hours. That year we witnessed several healing miracles as the presence of the Lord descended upon us as we worshiped and praised the living God.

Another time the Holy Spirit directed us to invite a prominent worship leader. We had a catered meal and retold the story of the Exodus from Egypt. The children searched our hall for a hidden piece of leavened bread, teaching them how leavening is like sin and how we must search ourselves diligently to root out all the sin in our lives. We then had Communion, and afterward, the worship leader led us in worship (song and dance) for several hours. People were supernaturally healed, and two people received Yeshua that night as their personal Savior. All we did was worship the God of Israel as He commanded us to do. I also have used items from the traditional Passover Seder to teach school groups how Yeshua was and is prophetically foreshadowed throughout Scripture.

OVERVIEW OF SHAVUOT

Chronologically, Shavuot (Pentecost), the Feast of Weeks, occurs next in the original Jewish calendar (Lev. 23:15–22). This special time takes place fifty days after the firstfruits ceremony. Along with other offerings, two loaves of leavened bread were presented to God. Deuteronomy 16:9–17 indicates that, although this festival accompanied the harvest, it was intended to remind us that we were once slaves in Egypt, before God set us free.

As our traditions developed, Shavuot became the festival of the giving of the Law. Evidently, the rabbis concluded by calculations that the giving of the Law at Mt. Sinai took place on this day. Traditional Jews read the scroll of Ruth in the synagogue on this day and occasionally refer to Shavuot as *Atzeret shel Pesach*, "the completion of Passover." Messianic significance abounds in this festival. From God's perspective, the time of great "harvest"—when large numbers of Jews and then Gentiles came into a personal relationship with Him—was initiated at the Shavuot after Yeshua's resurrection (Acts 2:40–43). The two leavened (impure) loaves of Shavuot *may* therefore symbolize Jew and Gentile "presented" to God and now part of His "family."

The apostle Paul's teaching about our former conditions as slaves to sin (Rom. 6–8) is certainly reminiscent of Shavuot's reminder that we were formerly slaves in Egypt. God set us free from slavery to sin by placing His Spirit in us to enable us to live as He intended (Rom. 8:1–4). God visibly placed His Spirit (Ruach

HaKodesh) in Yeshua's followers on that important Shavuot centuries ago (Acts 2:4).

Technically, the work of atonement is not complete unless man's sin nature (*yetzer hara*, "evil inclination") has been dealt with and power to overcome it has been granted. The coming of the Ruach HaKodesh served as the completion of Passover (Atzeret shel Pesach), the completion of our atonement, in the sense that through the Spirit God gives us the power we need to overcome our tendency toward evil. Yeshua Himself indicated this in John 16:7: "Unless I go away, the Counselor [Ruach HaKodesh] will not come to you; but if I go [i.e., "*firstfruits*," His resurrection], I will send him to you" (NIV). (Shavuot, the completion of the fifty days from firstfruits, occurs during Passover week.)

Shavuot possesses other Messianic significance as well. God spoke of a time when He would write His laws in our hearts (Jer. 31:32–33). Ezekiel 36:25–27 mentions His placing the Ruach in our hearts in this same connection. So God associates the giving of the Ruach with the placing of His Law in our hearts. What more appropriate time to visibly place His Ruach in His people than on Shavuot, the feast of the giving of the Law! Notice that Ezekiel connects the giving of the Ruach with the sprinkling of water on us. Moroccan Jews have an ancient custom they perform on Shavuot. They pour water on each other![4] This becomes one more symbol that Shavuot pictures God as visibly placing the Ruach in the followers of Yeshua.

HOW TO CELEBRATE SHAVUOT (PENTECOST)

As a congregation, we have started our Shavuot or Pentecost service with a processional. While playing slower music, we have a line of six to eight people walk into the sanctuary single file, each one carrying items such as a menorah, the Bible, sheaves of wheat, banners, the Israeli flag, or two loaves of bread. These items are laid upon the altar. We pray and then begin lively praise and worship. We are celebrating the giving of the Word, the Holy Spirit, and Yeshua—our Firstfruits!

Another year the Holy Spirit instructed us to set up a *Chupa* (wedding canopy) and place a large bronze pot under it to celebrate a rarely mentioned aspect of Pentecost. The Scripture tells us on Shavuot to give an offering according to how we have been blessed over the last year. This was a powerful act, because the Bible teaches that giving *is* worship! That Pentecost we received the largest offering God has ever given us!

Celebrate this wondrous and supernatural feast day in the Holy Spirit since this is when Father gave us the Ruach. Pray, fast, and ask the Holy Spirit for guidance! Have a Spirit-filled service; advertise in your local newspaper, on television, and on radio. Celebrate the two loaves of bread, Jew and Gentile, by hosting a "One New Man" celebration. Invite Jews and Gentiles to your Shavuot festival. Worship the God of Israel with lively music and dance, and be free in the Spirit. Worship and dance are powerful ways to involve all people, because these two acts tear down inhibitions in drawing close to God. We have so much for which to be thankful and joyous. God loves us so much that He gave us His Son and the Holy Spirit. This alone is reason enough for me to want to dance and celebrate.

The world is full of dead congregations and synagogues. We must invite His presence and be filled with His Spirit. There is nothing more powerful to an unbeliever than experiencing God's power and presence.

If you are not filled with the Holy Spirit, ask the Father in Yeshua's name for an infilling of the Holy Spirit! Pray in tongues and speak the Word of God! That is the theme of this holiday—the Word and the Holy Spirit. Peter submitted himself to the Holy Spirit over two thousand years ago (Acts 2), and three thousand Jews were saved! Be filled with the Holy Spirit, speak God's Word, and have three thousand people saved at your celebration! Walk in the anointing of the "One New Man."

OVERVIEW OF ROSH HASHANAH

This biblical holiday originated as "a sacred assembly, commemorated with trumpet blasts" (Lev. 23:23–25, NIV), a holy gathering. Today, we observe it as the New Year because, according to tradition, God created the world on this day. Rosh Hashanah is frequently called the day of remembrance (Yom HaZikaron) or the day of judgment (Yom HaDin) in view of its inauguration of the days of awe. The first name stresses God's faithfulness to His covenant and promises, the second His righteousness and justice. Still, the holiday conveys joy and delight, as illustrated by the custom of eating sweet things, such as apples dipped in honey.

A very interesting ceremony, *Tashlich*, grew up as part of the Rosh Hashanah observance. Devout Jews go to the edge of a body of water and empty their pockets or throw stones into the water. As they do this, they repeat Micah 7:18–20, which says, "You will...hurl all our iniquities into the depths of the sea" (NIV).

Since Rosh Hashanah originated as the memorial of blowing of trumpets, the shofar (or trumpet) plays an important role. Among other things it symbolizes, according to the rabbis, God's kingship and the coming of the Messianic Age (*Olam Haba*).

Rosh Hashanah has deep Messianic significance. The rabbis taught that one day the shofar would sound and the Messiah would come. When He came, the dead would rise.[5] About a decade after Yeshua, the apostle Paul talked about Messiah's return when he referred to the fact that Yeshua would return for His followers and would thereafter rule the earth as Messiah the King. People refer to this event as the Rapture or Yeshua's Second Coming. In describing the Rapture, Paul said, "For the Lord himself will come down from heaven, with a loud command, with the voice of the archangel and with the trumpet [shofar] call of God, and the dead in Christ will rise first" (1 Thess. 4:16, NIV). This day will certainly be characterized by joy, delight, and sweetness (cf. apples dipped in honey).

This particular resurrection is for those who have had, as Tashlich reminds us, their sins thrown into the sea by God because they have accepted Yeshua as Messiah. At this time, we will undergo a new "creation," so to speak (1 Cor. 15:50–53); we will receive new bodies. Remember, Rosh Hashanah traditionally commemorates the original creation. The Rapture, while being a sign of God's faithfulness to us (*Yom HaZikaron*, day of remembrance), ushers in a time of judgment on the world (*Yom HaDin*, day of judgment).

In Leviticus, the term *memorial* does not mean remembering something that is past. It calls attention to something about to occur. As we observe Rosh Hashanah, we should anticipate the time of Yeshua's return.

(How to celebrate a One New Man Rosh Hashanah service is found at the end of the Yom Kippur overview.)

OVERVIEW OF YOM KIPPUR

Leviticus 23:26–32 describes the Day of Atonement as a most solemn time of introspection and repentance. Those who did not observe this holy day were severely punished. On Yom Kippur only the high priest could enter the most sacred part of the sanctuary. After making a sacrifice for himself, he then brought the blood from the sacrifice that he made for the people (Leviticus 16). On this day, atonement was made for the *whole* nation, as a goat died in place of the people. (According to the most recent studies, *atonement* [in Hebrew, *kippur*] means "ransom by means of a substitute.")

Traditional observance has maintained the solemnity of this great day of repentance. Reminiscences of the Yom Kippur sacrifice still exist among some religious

Jews in the custom of *Kapporot*. A chicken is swung over the head as the following is recited: "This is my substitute, this is my commutation; this chicken goes to death; but may I be gathered and enter into a long and happy life and into peace."

Messianic significance abounds. The services during the period of Rosh Hashanah and Yom Kippur refer repeatedly to the binding or sacrifice of Isaac ("Akedah"). The rabbis teach that in some way God accepts the "sacrifice" of Isaac on our behalf. Isaac beautifully foreshadows the sacrifice of Messiah (see Hebrews 11:17–19), whose sacrifice God accepted on our behalf. The Haftorah portion on Yom Kippur is the Book of Jonah, the prophet who spent three days in the belly of a large fish before emerging. When Yeshua was challenged to provide evidence for His Messiahship, He pointed to the example of Jonah (Matt. 12:39–40). He used Jonah as a picture of His own death and resurrection. A *musaf* prayer found in many older Yom Kippur prayer books exhibits additional Messianic significance:

> The Messiah our righteousness has turned from us. We are alarmed, we have no one to justify us. Our sins and the yoke of our transgressions He bore. He was bruised for our iniquities. He carried on His shoulders our sins. With His stripes we are healed. Almighty God, hasten the day that He might come to us anew; that we may hear from Mt. Lebanon a second time through the Messiah ("Oz M'lifnai B'reshit").

The apostle Paul writes of a time in the future when all Israel will be redeemed and will have atonement (Rom. 11:26). The prophet Zechariah also predicted this time of national redemption (Zech. 12:10; 13:9). In the past, atonement was made for *all* Israel on Yom Kippur. Presently, this holy day looks forward to the time when *all* Israel will accept the atonement provided by the Messiah.

As we await this day, we can celebrate Yom Kippur by thanking God for the atonement available through Yeshua and by praying that more of our people will recognize and accept Him as their atonement. The tenor of the day also provides us with an opportunity for self-searching, repentance, and recommitment to God (cf. 2 Cor. 13:5; 1 John 1:9).

HOW TO CELEBRATE ROSH HASHANAH (NEW YEAR) AND YOM KIPPUR (DAY OF ATONEMENT)

We celebrate Rosh Hashanah and Yom Kippur as one holiday. We start by celebrating Rosh Hashanah with joy and anticipation of the coming of Messiah. We blow the shofar to start the service as Leviticus 23 commands us to do. We then worship the living God in celebratory song and dance. We sound the shofar repetitively as we pray over the congregation and individuals, breaking curses, diseases, and any other affliction upon them in the name of Yeshua. The shofar blast is like all the prophets of old proclaiming the promises of God. When the shofar is blown, we expect deliverances, healings, salvations, and miracles.

Yeshua shared in Matthew 24 that He would return with a great heavenly sounding of the shofar. Is this the memorial Leviticus 23 is talking about? Are we practicing, every Rosh Hashanah, the much anticipated great heavenly sounding of the shofar announcing the arrival of Yeshua's return?

Yeshua shared in Matthew that when He returns, He will judge the nations. Will Yeshua's judgment period take place during the "Ten Days of Awe" that fall between Rosh Hashanah and Yom Kippur?

Will the Yom Kippur that follows Yeshua's judgment period be the "Final Judgment," when our names are kept in or blotted out of the "Lamb's Book of Life"? Yeshua said that "no man knows the day or hour of My return, only the Father knows." When we celebrate Rosh Hashanah and Yom Kippur, we do it with a special feeling and sense of anticipated excitement, wondering: *When we blow the shofar this year, will we hear a great sounding from the heavens? Will Yeshua return this year?*

Between Rosh Hashanah and Yom Kippur, we fast together in unity as a congregation. We search ourselves for anything that is not of the Father and ask Him to remove it from us. We pray for unity among us as a body and ask God to make us the "One New Man." We pray as a corporate body for the salvation of Israel and the nations. This is also a perfect time to hold evangelistic meetings.

Then we celebrate Yom Kippur, which is traditionally one of the most somber feast days of the year. Yeshua is our High Priest who has gone into the holy of holies once and for all, opening the veil that allows us to have a personal relationship with our Father. We have had Jews visit our service on Yom Kippur and ask why we are so happy on such a somber day. What an opportunity to share Yeshua and bring them into the celebration, explaining that they have a sacrificial covering, His name is Yeshua, and we are happy and excited about it. We end our ten-day fast with the sounding of the shofar and teach from Hebrews 9. We celebrate the fact that our sins have been washed away. We then have Communion after worship to enter the holy of holies through the blood of Yeshua and spend time with our Father. That is the miracle of Yom Kippur!

OVERVIEW OF SUKKOT

Leviticus 23:43 portrays Sukkot (Festival of Booths or Tabernacles) as an eight-day period of rejoicing. Although it occurs at harvest time, the festival virtually ignores the harvest theme as it commemorates God's faithfulness to Israel through the wilderness wanderings after they left Egypt.

Traditional observance has maintained the spirit of great rejoicing during Sukkot. As in biblical times, meals are to be eaten in booths as a "picture of man's sojourn under God's wings" and also as a reminder of freedom from Egypt (Lev. 23:43). Participants carry the *lulav* branches and the *etrog* (a lemon-like fruit) in a procession through the synagogue and wave the branches in four directions. The waving of the branches goes back to earlier times when Near Eastern people welcomed visiting dignitaries in this way.

The seventh day of the celebration, Hoshana Rabba, gets its name from the prayers said on that day. Those prayers begin with the Hebrew *hoshana* ("save now") and include some special Messianic prayers. In tune with the spirit of joy, the participants recite Hallel psalms (113–118) during the week's celebration. It all culminates on the ninth day with Simchat Torah, the day of rejoicing over God's gift of the Law to the Jewish people.

During the second temple times, two events that no longer take place highlighted the celebration. Water, drawn from a nearby source, was brought to the temple and poured out by the altar as Isaiah 12:3 was repeated: "With joy you will draw water from the wells of salvation" (NIV). The torchlight parade, brilliantly illuminating the temple at night, stood out as the other great event, possibly reflecting a verse from one of the Hallel psalms: "The LORD is God, and he has made his light shine upon us" (Ps. 118:27, NIV).

Yeshua chose these two events to highlight His mission as Messiah. As the water was being poured by the altar, He announced, "If anyone is thirsty, let him come to me and drink. Whoever believes in me, as the Scripture has said, streams of living water will flow from within him" (John 7:37, NIV). As torches lit up the temple, He shouted, "I am the light of the world. Whoever follows me...will have the light of life" (John 8:12, NIV).

Messianic significance also abounds in the celebration as traditionally observed since temple days. Two verses from one of the Hallel psalms stand out: "The stone the builders rejected has become the capstone" (Ps. 118:22, NIV). This beautifully pictures the time when Yeshua will reign as Messiah, the King over the earth. The waving of the lulav, that oriental form of welcome, will be directed toward Him in that day. One of the prayers of Hoshana Rabba echoes this welcome to Messiah.

> "A voice heralds, heralds and saith: Turn unto Me and be ye saved, today if ye hear My voice. Behold the man who springs forth, Branch[6] is his name...."
>
> "But to His anointed, the Messiah, He giveth grace. Grant salvation to the eternal people. To David and to His seed[7] forever..."

This prayer eagerly anticipates the coming of the Messianic kingdom. Then, people will rejoice in the presence of the living Torah, Yeshua, the One called the Word of God (cf. John 1:1f). That Simchat Torah will have no rivals in its joy and celebration. (*Simchat Torah* means "rejoicing over the law" and occurs immediately following the Feast of Tabernacles.) Zechariah 14:16–19 describes this as a time when all nations, not just Israel, will keep the festival of Sukkot and live in booths.

As we celebrate Sukkot each year, we can anticipate that time when the booths will no longer picture our present "sojourn under God's wings." *Then* they will remind us of the past, *before* the reign of Yeshua HaMashiach the King. In the meantime, the booths remind us to depend on God and not on material goods (cf. Matt. 6:25–33).

HOW TO CELEBRATE SUKKOT (FEAST OF TABERNACLES)

Sukkot commemorates the forty-year period during which the children of Israel wandered in the desert, living in temporary shelters. During this festival, we build a *sukkah* (temporary shelter, booth) in our backyard. You can also put it on your balcony if you live in a multifamily home, such as an apartment. If neither of these are possibilities, you can share a sukkah with friends or family who do have one. Various plans to build a sukkah can be found in your local library or on the Internet. It is common practice, and highly commendable, to decorate your sukkah with seasonal decorations celebrating the harvest and God's provision. In the United States dried squash, corn, colorful fall foliage, grapes, and pumpkins are used to decorate the sukkah.

When seeing a decorated sukkah for the first time, Americans remark on how much it reminds them of the American holiday of Thanksgiving. The early settlers of America who began the Thanksgiving tradition were a deeply religious people. They looked to the Bible for guidance in expressing their gratitude to God for the bountiful harvest and their survival of another year in the new land. They based their early Thanksgiving celebrations in part on the biblical holiday of Sukkot.

Sukkot is our favorite feast day. In our backyard we build a large sukkah, approximately twelve feet by twelve feet, line the walls with bales of hay, outline the framework with strands of white holiday lights, and invite family, neighbors, and friends to worship in our sukkah every evening for the length of the feast.

Sukkot is the feast that we also celebrate the birth of Yeshua, who is the Son of the living God and who is our Salvation and Provision, our Shelter, and our Provider. It is so peaceful to sit in the sukkah on a beautiful fall evening with friends and family, worshiping God in song and dance, and rejoicing in the birth of our Messiah. This feast day is the most joyful of all.

In past years the Holy Spirit has led us to build a small sukkah in our sanctuary. We decorated it with brightly colored fall leaves, clusters of grapes, pumpkins, squash, and small bales of hay. As we danced and worshiped God, people were healed.

One woman was healed from colon cancer while dancing before the Lord. Another woman had endured several surgeries on her shoulder trying to resolve the constant pain issues. As she worshiped the Lord, the Holy Spirit touched her shoulder, and she immediately removed the sling she had been wearing for five months because she was healed!

One year we built our sukkah and placed a crib under it with baby Yeshua in it as our dance team danced to the song "Mary, Did You Know?" We then sang songs proclaiming our love and remembrance of God giving us Yeshua as our Messiah!

Invite unsaved Jewish and Gentile friends to

your services or home sukkah to dance and worship before the God of Israel! God moves mightily on His appointed times, His holy convocations. People will see Yeshua in these celebrations.

THE HOLIDAYS OUTSIDE THE LEVITICUS CYCLE

Overview of Purim

Purim commemorates the events of the scroll of Esther, as we relive our deliverance from Haman and take renewed faith in outliving the Hamans of other times. The celebration provides a joyous, carnival-type atmosphere.

Haman attempted to exterminate the Jews, so the holiday is a reminder of God's preservation of and commitment to Israel. But in the context of Purim, it reminds us of God's *preservation during our exile.* The disorderly, raucous, carnival nature of Purim then serves to remind us of God's preservation of our people through the years of exile until Messiah rules and disorder disappears.

How to celebrate Purim

Purim is a great way to teach others about God's plans and purposes for Israel despite anti-Semitism. We prepare to celebrate Purim as we do the feast days. We begin in prayer, seeking the leading of the Holy Spirit. We have previously hosted a Purim play, acting out the story of Purim, merging the traditional story with modern vernacular, dressing and portraying Haman as a terrorist or modern Middle Eastern dictator (it is open to interpretation). We had Queen Vashti act like a rebellious teenager, refusing to submit to authority, and portrayed Mordecai and Esther as godly examples of holiness and obedience, submitting themselves to God's will instead of their own will. It is a powerful message to Jew and Gentile alike.

The play provided a wonderful venue to teach children and adults God's plan for Israel, Jerusalem, and the prophetic importance of the Jewish people in the last days. It reemphasizes God's desire for us to stand with Israel and the Jewish people, even at the cost of our own lives. Mordecai's words spoken to Queen Esther are valid for all believers today: "Don't think for a moment that you will escape there in the palace when all other Jews are killed. If you keep quiet at a time like this, deliverance for the Jews will arise from some other place, but you and your relatives will die. What's more, who can say but that you have been elevated to the palace for just such a time as this?" (Esther 4:13–14, NLT).

We have also celebrated Purim by selecting seven or eight individuals to read an assigned portion from the Book of Esther before the congregation. We pass out noisemakers before the service. Whenever the name Haman is mentioned, the people are instructed to boo and hiss. When the name Mordecai is read, the congregation cheers and uses their noisemakers. This has such an impact on the children as they remain in the sanctuary for this reading. They listen intently to the story, waiting to hear the name of Mordecai or Haman mentioned. We conclude the reading with joyous praise and worship including dance. The people of

Israel are alive today because of divine intervention. What a tremendous reason to celebrate and worship the living God.

Overview of Hanukkah

Hanukkah reminds us of the victory won by the Maccabees in 165 B.C.E. to insure the purity of the worship of God and to preserve the distinctiveness of Israel and Jewish identity. After God granted this tremendous victory, the people cleansed and rededicated the temple. The Syrian ruler, Antiochus, had defiled the temple and turned it into a heathen shrine, hence the need for cleansing. Therefore, Hanukkah originated as the festival of the dedication or cleansing of the temple.

Yeshua used the Feast of Dedication (John 10:22) to proclaim Himself as the Good Shepherd (John 10:1ff). In the Jewish writings, shepherds frequently represented the leaders of Israel, both good and bad. (The Maccabees, for example, would have been considered among the good shepherds.) Yeshua, therefore, announced Himself as the Good Shepherd *par excellence*.

The Book of Daniel predicted the rise of Antiochus and his defiling of the temple (Daniel 8 and 11). Daniel also used Antiochus to represent a figure in the future whom Christian theologians call the Antichrist (Antimessiah). He will also defile the temple (in this case, the third temple, which is not yet built). The Antimessiah will cause great persecution for the Jewish people, a time known as Jacob's trouble (Jer. 30:4–7; cf. Zech. 13:8–9). At this time, Yeshua the Messiah, as the great Shepherd-leader (Zech. 12–14; cf. 1 Pet. 5:4), will come and win a tremendous victory, greater than that won by Yehudah the Maccabee. He will save Israel and establish His worldwide rule.

Hanukkah looks back to a victory and the preservation of the Jewish people when they were *in the land*. For us, it looks forward to a time when our Jewish people will be preserved despite intense suffering. This preservation, again while the Jewish people are in the land, will culminate in the victory won by the Great Shepherd, Yeshua.

Thus, Purim pictures our preservation from our enemies while we were in exile, and Hanukkah pictures our preservation while we were in the land. Both anticipate the reign of Messiah.

How to celebrate Hanukkah

Hanukkah is a story of miracles, sanctification, and salvation. What a fantastic time of year to share Yeshua. It is no accident that the Savior of the world was miraculously conceived during the Festival of Lights. We celebrated this miraculous holiday one year in worship and dance. Our dance team did the Hanukkah service, telling the story of Hanukkah and Yeshua through seven worship dance songs. In between the dances, a narrator shared stories of Hanukkah miracles from various periods of history such as the Holocaust, Russian pogroms, and the Maccabee period. We have had numerous visitors receive Yeshua at this holiday service as well. The only feast day celebration where we have had more people attend and receive Yeshua is at Passover. We advertised our Hanukkah service in our local newspaper and on the radio, bringing in Jew and Gentile, saved and unsaved alike. So many people are curious that they come by the hundreds to see what this holiday festival is all about.

One year a congregant wrote and directed a Hanukkah play, sharing the miraculous Hanukkah story and the correlation between the Festival of Lights and the Light of the World, Yeshua. This play touched many lives as they came to the altar to rededicate and cleanse their temples (their hearts) before God, and some received Yeshua. Again, these celebrations teach the children and provide an opportunity for the body to come together, worship, and remember all the miraculous things God has done for us!

FINAL THOUGHTS FROM RABBI ERIC CARLSON

Yeshua fulfilled the feast days so we can be free to enter the Father's presence and fellowship with Him, be filled with the Holy Spirit, and know God's will. God gave us the feast days to practice for the celebrations we will enjoy when we enter heaven. The feasts are a way to share Yeshua with both Jews and Gentiles. They are a prophetic vision of what is to come. When Yeshua returns, all nations will come to Jerusalem to celebrate the feast days. The feasts are our biblical culture that bind us together with Israel through shalom and unity in Yeshua. The feast days are God's and, in His words, are to be celebrated forever. Celebrate the feasts filled with the Holy Spirit, as the One New Man—Yeshua!

After every feast day or holiday celebration, we *oneg*, or have "holiday delight." How do we do oneg? We prepare traditional holiday or feast-day food items (mostly potluck, families will bring in their favorite holiday recipe). We decorate a fellowship hall according to the current holiday theme. On Hanukkah we use a lot of candles. For Sukkot we use fall foliage, pumpkins, and gourds. We then invite everyone who attended the service to this hall to oneg with us—to fellowship with one another and eat. We have had numerous people attend our celebration services then come and oneg with us, asking questions one-on-one in the fellowship hall (a very unimposing room) and then receive Yeshua. Oneg provides a comfortable, family atmosphere where people feel very relaxed and open to discuss and ask questions about Yeshua. Oneg helps us reclaim the fellowship and intimacy of personal interaction that has been lost to an impersonal, electronic society.

In Your Search for the Truth

The Scripture quotations used below were taken from the Holy Bible, New International Version. Copyright © 1973, 1978, 1984, International Bible Society. Used by permission.

The Bible Is True

These scriptures will help you to establish the truth of God's Word. All prophecies are from the Jewish Scriptures.

Preservation of the Jewish people

This is what the LORD says,

he who appoints the sun
    to shine by day,
who decrees the moon and stars
    to shine by night,
who stirs up the sea
    so that its waves roar—

the LORD Almighty is his name:
"Only if these decrees vanish from my sight,"
    declares the LORD,
"will the descendants of Israel ever cease
    to be a nation before me."
                    —JEREMIAH 31:35–36

Dispersion of the Jewish people

You who were as numerous as the stars in the sky
will be left but few in number, because you did
not obey the LORD your God.... Then the LORD
will scatter you among all nations, from one end
of the earth to the other. There you will worship
other gods—gods of wood and stone, which neither you nor your fathers have known.
                    —DEUTERONOMY 28:62, 64

Survival of the Jewish people

Yet in spite of this, when they are in the land of
their enemies, I will not reject them or abhor
them so as to destroy them completely, breaking
my covenant with them. I am the LORD their
God.
                    —LEVITICUS 26:44

Formation of Israel and the regathering of the Jewish people

In that day the Lord will reach out his hand a
second time to reclaim the remnant that is left
of his people.... He will raise a banner for the
nations and gather the exiles of Israel; he will

assemble the scattered people of Judah from the four quarters of the earth.

—ISAIAH 11:11–12

Israel rebuilt

They will rebuild the ruined cities and live in them.

—AMOS 9:14

Agricultural achievements

The desert and the parched land will be glad; the wilderness will rejoice and blossom.

—ISAIAH 35:1

Jerusalem: A burden for all people

I am going to make Jerusalem a cup that sends all the surrounding peoples reeling. Judah will be besieged as well as Jerusalem. On that day, when all the nations of the earth are gathered against her, I will make Jerusalem an immovable rock for all the nations. All who try to move it will injure themselves.

—ZECHARIAH 12:2–3

All nations will turn against Israel

I will gather all nations to Jerusalem to fight against it.

—ZECHARIAH 14:2

"In the whole land," declares the LORD, "two-thirds will be struck down and perish."
—ZECHARIAH 13:8

SHALOM WITH GOD

Do the Jewish Scriptures talk about life after death? Daniel says:

Multitudes who sleep in the dust of the earth will awake: some to everlasting life, others to shame and everlasting contempt.
—DANIEL 12:2

How can we awake to everlasting life? By not being separated from God. The Bible says all of us are separated from God. We read in Psalm 14:3:

All have turned aside,
    they have together become corrupt;
there is no one who does good,
    not even one.

And in Isaiah 59:2:

But your iniquities have separated
    you from your God.

God gave us a way of "covering our sins" (atonement) through the sacrifice of an unblemished animal in the temple:

It is the blood that makes atonement for one's life.

—LEVITICUS 17:11

Since the temple was destroyed in A.D. 70, animal sacrifices for atonement are impossible. How can we have the blood of atonement today?

Jeremiah predicted a New Covenant for the house of Israel and Judah:

"The time is coming," declares the LORD,
"when I will make a new covenant
with the house of Israel...
and will remember their sins no more."

—JEREMIAH 31:31, 34

God provided this New Covenant blood of atonement through a perfect sacrificial Lamb, one called "The Messiah." Isaiah described how to recognize Him:

Who has believed our message
and to whom has the arm of the LORD been
revealed?...
He had no beauty or majesty to attract us to
him, nothing in his appearance that we
should desire him.
He was despised and rejected by men,
a man of sorrows, and familiar with suffering.
Like one from whom men hide their faces
he was despised, and we esteemed him not.

Surely he took up our infirmities
and carried our sorrows,
yet we considered him stricken by God,
smitten by him, and afflicted.
But he was pierced for our transgressions,
he was crushed for our iniquities;
the punishment that brought us peace was upon
him,
and by his wounds we are healed.
We all, like sheep, have gone astray,
each of us has turned to his own way;
and the LORD has laid on him
the iniquity of us all.
—ISAIAH 53:1–6

God made sure we could recognize the Messiah by giving us over three hundred identifying marks as described by the prophets of Israel. Below are a few of them.

He would be born in Bethlehem of Judah.

But you, Bethlehem Ephrathah, though you are
small among the clans of Judah,
out of you will come for me
one who will be ruler over Israel,
whose origins are from of old,
from ancient times.
—MICAH 5:2

His ancestry was to be of the family of David.

"The days are coming," declares the LORD,
    "when I will raise up to David a righteous
        Branch....
This is the name by which he will be called:
    The LORD Our Righteousness."
                                    —JEREMIAH 23:5–6

The Gentiles will follow Him.

In that day the Root of Jesse will stand as a banner for the peoples; the nations will rally to him,
and his place of rest will be glorious.
                                    —ISAIAH 11:10

He was to die *before* the second temple was destroyed.

After the sixty-two "sevens," the Anointed One
will be cut off and will have nothing. The people
of the ruler who will come will destroy the city
[Jerusalem] and the sanctuary. [The temple was
destroyed in A.D. 70.]
                                    —DANIEL 9:26

Since God has provided the blood of atonement
through Messiah Yeshua (Jesus), we must repent (admit
we have sinned and turn from unrighteousness) and ask
for forgiveness in the name of Yeshua. Each individual's
prayer should be:

Messiah Yeshua, I admit that I have sinned. I believe that You have provided the blood of atonement for me. I receive You now as my Messiah and Lord. Thank You for giving me shalom with God.

DIALOGUE

I was born a Jew, and I will die a Jew!

You do not give up your Jewish identity to receive Yeshua. On the contrary, you gain a personal relationship with the God of Abraham, Isaac, and Jacob through your walk with the Jewish Messiah.

Doesn't belief in Yeshua mean that you are no longer Jewish?

This question really is not the issue. The question "How can you be Jewish and believe in Yeshua?" is better answered with another question: "Who is Yeshua?"

If Yeshua, as claimed, is Israel's promised Messiah, then, according to the Scriptures, in order to be a truly observant Jew, one must acknowledge and believe in Yeshua as the Messiah.

One is either Jewish or Gentile by birth—nothing can change that. According to the Bible, a Jew is a person who is descended from Abraham, Isaac, and Jacob.

Yeshua and His earliest followers were Jewish. They never renounced their Jewish heritage, nor were they expected to do so. Believing in—and trusting—the Jewish Messiah can add to one's appreciation of Judaism.

We Jews believe in one God, not three.

Followers of Yeshua also believe in one God, not three. Most Jews recite the Shema, the Jewish confession of faith, "Hear O Israel, the Lord our God, *the Lord is one.*" However, the translation of the New Jewish Version, recognized as the most accurate English translation produced by Jewish scholars, states: "Hear O Israel, the Lord is our God, *the Lord alone.*" The point of the Shema is to demand absolute faith in the Lord alone, with no gods before Him. The Hebrew word *echad*, translated "alone" here, means "one" in the sense of "that one alone."

In the twelfth century, Moses Maimonides, writing to counter Christian and Muslim beliefs, compiled his thirteen articles of faith, recited by observant Jews daily. One of the articles states that Jews must believe that God is *yachid* or "absolute unity." But this is unscriptural, since the Hebrew Bible gives clear indications of God's composite unity.

Genesis 19:24 states that "the LORD rained down burning sulfur on Sodom and Gomorrah, from the LORD out of the heavens." In other words, the Lord, *who had been on the earth talking to Abraham* (read Genesis 18:1–33 very carefully) rained down fire and brimstone from the Lord *out of the heavens.*

The Spirit of God came upon many people in the Scriptures. For instance, Isaiah 61:1 states, "The Spirit of the Sovereign LORD is on me."

And, finally, who is God's *Son* in Proverbs 30:4?

Who has gone up to heaven and come down?
Who has gathered up the wind in the hollow
of his hands?
Who has wrapped up the waters in his cloak?
Who has established all the ends of the earth?
What is his name, and the name of his son?
Tell me if you know!

Isaiah 42:1 speaks of God's Servant (that is, the Messiah) upon whom God places His Spirit so that "he will bring justice to the nations." Here in one passage is a reference to the Lord (the Father), the Messiah (the Son), and the Spirit.

Here is my servant, whom I uphold,
my chosen one in whom I delight;
I will put my Spirit on him
and he will bring justice to the nations.

Jewish people don't need a middleman.

Judaism historically has required a priesthood, the Levites, to minister between the Israelites and their holy God. Leviticus 1:15 directed that only a priest (one of Aaron's sons) could sprinkle the blood of atonement in the Tent of Meeting for the forgiveness of sin.

Followers of Yeshua now have direct access to God through the mediatorial role performed by Jesus. We now approach the Lord directly and go right into His holy presence. No Jew in Bible days, aside from the high priest (and at that, only once a year), could ever do this.

Jewish people do not believe in human sacrifice.

Followers of Yeshua do not believe in this either. We as human beings have no right to sacrifice another human being for our sins. Only God has the absolute right to give life and take it away. Because the penalty for sin is death (Ezek. 18:4), God, in His great mercy, provided His own sacrifice to pay for the sins of the world. His own Son willingly suffered the death penalty for us.

It is the absolutely clear teaching of Isaiah 53 that God would place the punishment due His people upon an innocent and righteous sufferer who would die for Israel's sins. Yeshua the Messiah fulfilled this prophecy.

Judaism does not believe in original sin.

Depending on one's definition of original sin, one may say that Judaism does or does not believe in this teaching. Psalm 51:5, which states, "Surely I was sinful at birth, sinful from the time my mother conceived me," clearly teaches the inherent sinfulness of man. And, according to some Jewish traditions, all human souls were in Adam when he sinned. Thus, when Adam sinned, the entire human race fell with him.

There can be no question, however, that the Hebrew Bible teaches the *universality* of sin. Genesis 8:21 says that "every inclination [Hebrew, *yetzer*] of [man's] heart is evil from childhood." And Ecclesiates 7:20 says, "There is not a righteous man on earth who does what is right and never sins." Proverbs 20:9 asks, "Who can say, 'I have kept my heart pure; I am clean and without sin'?" And Isaiah 53:6 states that "we all, like sheep, have gone astray, each of us has turned to his own way." The sinfulness of man is clearly taught throughout the entire Hebrew Bible.

Religions are all alike. They all have some good points and can help people to lead worthwhile lives.

Faith in the Messiah is not a religion; it is God's declared way for mankind to be reconciled to Him. While there are many good points to commend in some religions, this does not mean that God is satisfied with everything in "religion."

What is important is not what man decides about God, but rather what God decides about man. We must approach God according to *His* standards. It is not up to us to devise our own way of approaching Him. Since He has given us a way to have our sins forgiven, then it is our *privilege* to accept His grace.

Why did God allow six million Jews to die in the Holocaust?

> The secret things belong to the LORD our God,
> but the things revealed belong to us.
> —DEUTERONOMY 29:29

God has chosen to keep some of the reasons for the Holocaust a mystery. But some reasons have been revealed.

God tells us that if we obeyed the law, we would be a nation of priests and blessed above all people on the face of the earth. However, if we violated the law, we would lose our homeland and be scattered to the four corners of the earth. And wherever we would go, we would be persecuted (Deut. 28).

It was as if God's law was a picket fence of protection around us. However, once we went out of the gate of protection, we would be destroyed.

In addition to this warning in His Word, God always sent prophets calling for repentance in the hope judgment could be averted. Sometimes we repented as the Ninevites did when warned by Jonah, and sometimes we ignored God's message, as in Jerusalem when Jeremiah warned of Nebuchadnezzar's invasion. Before the Holocaust of Hitler, God warned us through fiery zionists like Theodor Herzl and Ze'ev Jabotinsky. In 1938, Jabotinsky said, "I see a horrible vision. Time is growing short for you to be spared."[1]

Even with the warnings, why a God of love allowed the Holocaust is a secret we will not fully understand until we get to heaven.

What happens to Jews who do not believe in Jesus?

The only way to be granted forgiveness of sin is belief in Yeshua. Yeshua said, "Hear, O Israel, the Lord our God, the Lord is one" (Mark 12:29). This is called the Shema and is chanted by God-fearing Jews.

, Jeremiah 29:13 says, "You will seek me and find me when you seek me with all your heart."

Some believe that many Jews, sincerely seeking God, died with the Shema on their lips and had revelations of Yeshua in concentration camps and during other times of trial and tribulation.

Only God knows those who are seeking Him with

all their hearts. We cannot know what is in any heart but our own. Who do *you* say Yeshua is?

Christians have always hated and persecuted the Jewish people.

Not everyone who calls himself a Christian *is* a Christian. Yeshua, who commanded His followers to love all men, said:

> Watch out for false prophets. They come to you in sheep's clothing, but inwardly they are ferocious wolves. By their fruit you will recognize them.
> —MATTHEW 7:15–16

If a person does not bear the Christian "fruit" of love, compassion, and mercy, then he has no right to call himself a Christian.

Do Jewish people need to repent?

The Hebrew word for "repent" is *shuv* (pronounced *shoov*), and it literally means, "turn, turn back." Many times God spoke through His prophets to Israel saying, "Turn back to Me and I will turn back to you." (See Zechariah 1:3–4; Joel 2:12–14.) In other words, if Israel would *repent*, then God would *relent*.

But do Jews need to "turn back" today? The answer is emphatically "Yes!" since all Jews are members of the human race; all human beings sin; whoever sins "turns away" from God; and whoever has "turned away" needs to "turn back"!

Have you sinned in thought, word, or deed? Have you stolen something, committed a lustful act, hated someone in your heart, displayed ingratitude, abused your body, told a lie, or been filled with pride? Is there any way at all, be it large or small, that you have turned away from God? Then whoever you are, Jew or Gentile, you need to repent ("turn back")!

Doesn't Isaiah 53 refer to the Jewish people as a whole?

The earliest Jewish interpretations of chapter 53, which really begins with Isaiah 52:13, said that it spoke of Messiah. It is clear for many reasons that it *cannot* refer to the Jewish people as a whole, or even to a righteous remnant within the nation. This passage also *cannot* refer to a "Messianic Age" because verse 3 would then have the people reject a utopia: "He was despised and rejected by men, a man of sorrows...." Furthermore, Israel has never been a silent sufferer: "...yet he did not open his mouth" (v. 7). And, who is "my people" if "he" refers to Israel? "For he was cut off from the land of the living; for the transgression of my people he was stricken" (v. 8).

The prophet Hosea describes Israel as a harlot; Israel, unlike the Messiah described in the passage, is *not* without sin: "...nor was any deceit in his mouth" (Isa. 53:9).

Furthermore, according to the Torah, the Jewish people would only suffer if they were *un*righteous. Nowhere is it ever taught that Israel would suffer for the sins of the world. Only Jesus has ever fulfilled this prophecy.

Notes

CHAPTER 2
THE RABBINIC CONSPIRACY

1. As cited in Kevin Howard and Marvin Rosenthal, *The Feasts of the Lord* (Nashville: Thomas Nelson Publishers, 1997), 126.
2. Dan Gruber, *Rabbi Akiba's Messiah* (Hanover, NH: Elijah Publishing, 1999), 80. Gruber's book provides an excellent history of the origins of Rabbinic Judaism.
3. Ibid.
4. Erubin 21b in J. M. Baumgarten, "The Unwritten Law in the Pre-Rabbinic Period," *Journal for the Study of Judaism in the Persian, Hellenistic and Roman Period*, vol. III (October 1972): 23, as cited in Gruber, 107.
5. Gruber, 111, 116–118.
6. Raymond Robert Fischer, *Full Circle* (Tiberias, Israel: Olim Publications, 2002), 56.

7. Ron Cantor, *I Am Not Ashamed* (Gaithersburg, MD: Tikkun International, 1999), 140–141.

8. Ibid., 142.

9. For the commentaries of the rabbis before Yeshua and the revisionary views of the modern rabbis on the major Messianic prophecies, read Philip Moore, *The End of History, Messiah Conspiracy* (Atlanta: Ramshead Press International, 1996).

CHAPTER 3
WHO IS ISRAEL?

1. Derek Prince, *Prophetic Destinies* (Altamonte Springs, FL: Creation House, 1992), 13.

2. See the Foreword to Sid Roth, *Time Is Running Short* (Shippensburg, PA: Destiny Image Publishers, 1990).

3. Over the years some have objected to my use of the term "Gentile Christian." I meet many Christians who are ashamed of their Gentile heritage and wish they were Jewish. Some feel that the term *Gentile* is even derogatory. While the word *Gentiles* has sometimes been associated with "heathen," it is better defined as "nations" or "non-Jews"—a distinct people group. The term is neutral. There are good Gentiles and bad Gentiles, just as there are good Jews and bad Jews. Besides, Paul would not have addressed non-Jewish believers as "Gentiles" if it were an insult. (See Romans 11:13; 16:4; and Galatians 2:12, 14.)

Should we let unbelievers define our identity? Although I am a new creation in Yeshua, I am not ashamed of my Jewish heritage. If I were a Gentile, I would not be ashamed of my Gentile heritage. But I would be proud of my identity. Our *heritage* is Jewish or Gentile, but our *identity* is Yeshua!

CHAPTER 5
CHRISTIAN?

1. One example of a church leader who stood up for the Jewish people was Dietrich Bonhoeffer, a German Lutheran minister whose refusal to recant his opposition to Adolph Hitler's Nazi regime led to his imprisonment and eventual execution. He openly opposed not only the Nazi's anti-Jewish policies but also the church's acquiescence to those policies.
2. Unless otherwise noted, the following historical references are from Steffi Rubin, *Anti-Semitism* (N.p.: Hineni Ministries, 1977), 32–33.
3. As cited in X. Malcolm Hay, *Europe and the Jews* (Boston: Beacon Press, 1961), 27.
4. F. E. Talmage, ed., *Disputation and Dialogue: Readings in the Jewish-Christian Encounter* (New York: Ktav Publishing House, Inc., 1975), 18.
5. As cited in *Encyclopaedia Judaica* (Jerusalem: Keter Publishing House Jerusalem Ltd., 1972), vol. 8, 692.
    Luther instructed "rulers who have Jewish subjects [to] exercise a sharp mercy toward these wretched people.... They must act like a good physician who, when gangrene has set in, proceeds without mercy to cut, saw, and burn flesh, veins, bone, and marrow.... Burn down their synagogues.... If this does not help we must drive them out like mad dogs." From *Luther's Works, Vol. 47: The Christian in Society IV* (Philadelphia: Fortress Press, 1971), 268–293. Excerpts cited in the Internet Medieval Sourcebook at www.fordham .edu/halshall/source/luther-jews.html.
6. *Encyclopaedia Judaica*, vol. 8, 693.
7. Adolph Hitler, *Mein Kampf*, translated by Ralph Manheim (Boston: Houghton Mifflin Co., 1971), 65.
8. True repentance is not just saying you are sorry. It involves a change of behavior.

CHAPTER 6
THE CONSTANTINE CONSPIRACY

1. Raymond Robert Fischer, *The Children of God: Messianic Jews and Gentile Christians Nourished by Common Jewish Roots* (Tiberias, Israel: Olim Publications, 2000), 47.
2. Theodoret, *Historia Ecclesiastica 1*, 10.
3. Lars Enarson, "The Feast of Passover and Intercession for Salvation of the Jewish People: An Appeal for an All Night Prayer Vigil on April 7 or 8, 2001" (The Watchman International, P. O. Box 3670, Pensacola, FL 32516, 1999), 1–2.
4. "In the fifth century the western church [Roman Catholic] ordered it to be celebrated forever on the day of the old Roman feast of the birth of Sol [sun]" *The Encyclopedia Americana*, 1942 Edition, vol. 6, 623.
5. *Century Dictionary and Cyclopedia*, 1903, vol. 2, 987.
6. Tertullian, *Against Marcion 1*, ANF III, 271.
7. *Dialogue 21,*1; 23,3.
8. See Fischer's book *The Children of God* for a more detailed history of the first church.

CHAPTER 7
BIBLICAL FESTIVALS—BLESSING OR BONDAGE?

1. A traditional understanding of the Passover seder ties the four cups of wine to the four "I will" statements of Exodus 6:6–7: "Therefore say to the children of Israel: 'I am the Lord; I will bring you out from under the burdens of the Egyptians, I will rescue you from their bondage, and I will redeem you with an outstretched arm and with great judgments. I will take you as My people, and I will be your God. . . .'" "I will redeem you" is the third statement, which corresponds to the third cup.

CHAPTER 8
THE LAW OF EVANGELISM

1. John Owen quoted in *A Puritan Golden Treasury*, compiled by I. D. E. Thomas (Carlisle, PA: Banner of Truth, 1977) 155, 157 as cited in Michael Brown, *Our Hands Are Stained with Blood* (Shippensburg, PA: Destiny Image, 1992), 20.

CHAPTER 11
TRUTH OR CONSEQUENCES

1. John McTernan, *God's Final Warning to America* (Oklahoma City, OK: Hearthstone Publishing, 2000), 82–119.
2. Timothy Snodgrass, "History and Future of USS New Madrid," http://www.etpv.org/2002/histand.html (accessed May 19, 2004).
3. Ibid.
4. Seth Gitell, "Clinton's Ambition, Arafat's War," http://www.providencephoenix.com/archive/features/00/10/19/MIDEAST.html (accessed May 19, 2004).

APPENDIX B
CELEBRATE THE FEASTS

1. Dr. John Fischer, *The Meaning and Importance of the Jewish Holidays*, copyright © 1979. For more information, contact Menorah Ministries, P. O. Box 669, Palm Harbor, FL 34682.
2. There is ample indication that Yeshua Himself probably instituted this practice, which then found its way into traditional observance because of the early Messianic Jews.
3. C. F. Lampe, *A Patristic Greek Lexicon*.

4. See Hayyim Schauss, *The Jewish Festivals: A Guide to Their History and Observance* (New York: Schocken Books, 1996), 95.
5. For more information, read Joseph Hertz's book *Daily Prayer Book*, 865.
6. Both are references to Messiah, the seed and branch of David (cf. Isa. 9:5–6; Jer. 23:5–6).
7. See endnote above.

APPENDIX C
IN YOUR SEARCH FOR THE TRUTH

1. Shmuel Katz, *Lone Wolf: A Biography of Vladimir (Ze'ev) Jabotinky* (New York: Barricade Books, 1996), as quoted in *Jerusalem Post*, "Books on the Shoah That Make the Difference," *Jerusalem Post*, Internet edition (May 8, 2000): http://www.jpost.com/Editions/2000/05/01/ Books/Books.6034.html (accessed June 14, 2004).

Write for our free newsletter and catalog:

Messianic Vision
P. O. Box 1918
Brunswick, GA 31521-1918
(912) 265-2500
(912) 265-3735 (fax)
E-mail: info@sidroth.org

See our television program and hear our radio show
twenty-four hours a day at www.sidroth.org.

Strang Communications, the publisher of both Charisma House and *Charisma* magazine, wants to give you a FREE SUBSCRIPTION to our award-winning magazine.

Since its inception in 1975, Charisma magazine has helped thousands of Christians stay connected with what God is doing worldwide.

Within its pages you will discover in-depth reports and the latest news from a Christian perspective, biblical health tips, global events in the body of Christ, personality profiles, and so much more. Join the family of *Charisma* readers who enjoy feeding their spirit each month with miracle-filled testimonies and inspiring articles that bring clarity, provoke prayer, and demand answers.

To claim your **3 free issues** of *Charisma*, send your name and address to: Charisma 3 Free Issue Offer, 600 Rinehart Road, Lake Mary, FL 32746. Or you may call 1-800-829-3346 and ask for Offer # 93FREE. This offer is only valid in the USA.

---

www.charismamag.com

3581